As we draw closer to the return of the Lord, spiritual warfare will intensify. Those who oppose God will be stronger and more malevolent than ever before, and those who serve Him will experience an intensification of God's miraculous power as never before. Paul said, be filled with the Holy Spirit. Jesus said, you will receive power after the Holy Spirit has come upon you and you will be my witnesses. There is no way the Church can go forth and witness to the unconverted world without the power of God. There is no way that Christians can go forth into the spiritual battle without the power of the Holy Spirit. In *The Supernatural Life*, Cindy Jacobs bridges the natural and supernatural. Read the book, receive the power, and live the supernatural life.

PAT ROBERTSON
Founder and Chairman, The Christian Broadcasting Network
Host, *The 700 Club*
Author, *Bring It On* and *Courting Disaster*

Breakthrough is occurring in the spirit realm around us and it is the prelude to change in the natural world in which we live. We need supernatural strength at this critical crossroads in history. Are you satisfied living within the limitations of the natural realm? Or do you want to move forward in faith? Cindy Jacobs knows the way because she has lived the supernatural life. In this book, she has woven a compelling tapestry of the great heritage of believers who have been empowered in the past and God's desire to release His anointing today. This is a must-read for everyone who wants to tap into the supernatural realm while living in the natural realm.

DUTCH SHEETS
Author, *Hope Resurrected* and *History Makers*

Cindy's new book is riveting. My heart burned as I read it. I felt a switch turn on in my heart—with a desire to seek more of the Spirit's power in my own life and to pursue healing prayers for others. I pray that this is more than a mere book—that it becomes a tool of the Holy Spirit to reach out to ignite the hearts of thousands upon thousands with a desire to seek the Lord strongly.

STEVE SJOGREN
Pastor, Vineyard Community Church, Cincinnati, Ohio
Author, *Changing the World Through Kindness* and *Community of Kindness*

Cindy Jacobs shows believers how to live in the arena of the miraculous and gives us practical steps that will help sharpen our God-given gifts. Why settle for less than God's best? I highly recommend *The Supernatural Life* for people desiring to break out of the ordinary and live the extraordinary life God has destined for them!

BARBARA WENTROBLE
Founder, International Breakthrough Ministries
Author, *Prophetic Intercession, You Are Anointed* and *God's Purpose for Your Life*

Many people are calling this new era "The Day of the Saints." Cindy has done a great job explaining how ordinary people become extraordinary Christians, doing the works of Jesus. This is a down-to-earth manual for moving in gifts with lots of real-life examples. I love it!

BARBARA J. YODER
Senior Pastor, Shekinah Christian Church
National Apostolic Council, United States Strategic Prayer Network
Author and Speaker

THE SUPER- NATURAL LIFE

CINDY JACOBS

Regal

From Gospel Light
Ventura, California, U.S.A.

PUBLISHED BY REGAL BOOKS
FROM GOSPEL LIGHT
VENTURA, CALIFORNIA, U.S.A.
PRINTED IN THE U.S.A.

Regal Books is a ministry of Gospel Light, a Christian publisher dedicated to serving the local church. We believe God's vision for Gospel Light is to provide church leaders with biblical, user-friendly materials that will help them evangelize, disciple and minister to children, youth and families.

It is our prayer that this Regal book will help you discover biblical truth for your own life and help you meet the needs of others. May God richly bless you.

For a free catalog of resources from Regal Books/Gospel Light, please call your Christian supplier or contact us at 1-800-4-GOSPEL *or* www.regalbooks.com.

Cover design by David Griffing
Edited by Steven Lawson

Library of Congress Cataloging-in-Publication Data
Jacobs, Cindy.
    The supernatural life / Cindy Jacobs.
      p. cm.
    Includes index.
    ISBN 0-8307-3703-0 (hard cover)
    1. Gifts, Spiritual. 2. Christian life. I. Title.
    BT767.3.J33 2005
    234'.13—dc22   2005003629

1   2   3   4   5   6   7   8   9   10   /   10   09   08   07   06   05

Rights for publishing this book in other languages are contracted by Gospel Light Worldwide, the international nonprofit ministry of Gospel Light. Gospel Light Worldwide also provides publishing and technical assistance to international publishers dedicated to producing Sunday School and Vacation Bible School curricula and books in the languages of the world. For additional information, visit www.gospellightworldwide.org; write to Gospel Light Worldwide, P.O. Box 3875, Ventura, CA 93006; or send an e-mail to info@gospellightworldwide.org.

THIS BOOK IS DEDICATED

TO THE LOVE OF MY LIFE,

MIKE JACOBS

CONTENTS

ACKNOWLEDGEMENTS

I want to thank the Lord for helping me with the writing of this book. Each book seems to have its challenges and this was both a joy and a battle.

Thank you, Mike, Madison and Daniel. I am so glad that you are my family.

Praise God for my prayer partners. I know that I thank you in each book, but I wouldn't finish any book without you. Thanks to my sister, Lucy Reithmiller, and my friend Cheryl Sacks. You have been particularly encouraging.

Special thanks go to the staff at Generals International for standing with me in this writing. Laura Baca lovingly stepped in to do the index for me at the last minute. Thank you! Great will be your reward in heaven!

I also want to acknowledge Steven Lawson as the editor who has been so helpful to me and Bayard Taylor who helped me explain some complicated points. In addition, I want to express my gratitude to Bill Greig III, Kim Bangs and everyone at Regal Books who love me and stand with me both in relationship and prayer. You are the best!

Thank you, Carmen, for cleaning my house, and thank you, Beth Moore, for coming over to help me time and again when I get bogged down with everyday life. I love you both.

THE SUPERNATURAL JOURNEY

When I was a new Christian, my friends and I formed a group called the God Squad. Many of us looked a bit strange. The guys wore their hair long (young Christians who do that today are sometimes called Nazirites[1]), and the girls mostly parted their hair down the middle and wore it straight and long.

We were wildly radical for Jesus. We spent many Saturdays knocking on the doors of people we didn't know, seeking those who needed an encounter with Jesus. We spent countless hours praying to God for those who needed His healing touch. And we spent numerous days telling of the Holy Spirit's power and how He had transformed our lives. People who had been lost were found; the sick were healed; and the power came. We did not know that we were in a time of God's visitation; we just lived supernaturally natural lives. It was the best of times. We were Jesus Freaks!

We Are on the Threshold of a Fresh Visitation

God is again coming with great waves of glory to touch the world. All across the face of the earth the prophets are saying that we are moving into a tremendous time of signs and wonders such as the world has never experienced. This move of the Holy Spirit will be accompanied by a great and mighty harvest of souls. God is moving on college campuses, in neighborhoods and in cities. There is a fresh longing in God's people to be used by Him to share the Good News of salvation to heal the blind and to raise the dead.

None of us wants to miss this move of God. I have written this book not only to tell about what we experienced as Jesus Freaks but also to show what everyone can expect and experience today.

I realize that in order for this move to take place, there needs to be a connection between those who have blazed a trail before us and the generations of today. While many members of my generation remember God's visitation in the 1970s, it was not God's first big move. Before Jesus freaks came along, there were great believers such as Smith Wigglesworth, Aimee Semple McPherson, Charles Finney, Jonathan Edwards and Kathryn Kuhlman. The list is long and stretches back to Paul, Peter and all of the Early Church's disciples. In fact, it really goes back to the Jewish patriarchs, including Moses, Abraham and Elijah. We stand upon their shoulders in the area of knowledge and revelation concerning signs and wonders.

This Book Is for You!

This is a fun book. It is one that everyone will enjoy reading. God just loves to cause His creation to pause and marvel at the millions upon millions of ways that He is a supernatural God.

For those in the Charismatic/Pentecostal stream, this book will be a reminder to go back to the first things some of us have learned from such times as the Jesus People Movement. For those who believe in God, but have never experienced the supernatural firsthand, this book will not only introduce you to the supernatural life but will also plant within you a desire to live it. For anyone who does not believe in God, or is not sure about spiritual matters, you may not understand everything in this book, but go ahead and read it anyway—you will get a peak at some of God's greatness and will probably want to explore more.

While I include some context, the purpose of this book is not to explain the theological details of healing, speaking in tongues or any of

God's miraculous acts. At the back, I provide a recommended reading list of books that give full explanations and further insight. Here, I have written mostly about my adventures, the experiences of others and what you can expect in the days ahead. This is not a textbook per se; rather, I start from the point of believing in a supernatural God who enables us to live supernatural lives.

Enjoy this book. Let it stretch you to a fresh hunger to be used of God. Laugh with me as you experience my journey. Take out a pen and join in the action by answering the questions at the end of each chapter and journaling in the space provided. Engage yourself with the almighty God of the universe who wants to use you as His supernatural ambassador to the world. Then go out and release the power of a loving God to your generation.

CHAPTER ONE

SUPERNATURALLY NATURAL

Once when my children were small, we were visiting Los Angeles. Both Daniel and Madison were acting their age: They were poking each other and saying things such as "Mom, he looked at me" and "Mom, she breathed on me!" Before I returned our rental car I had to fill it up with gasoline. As I pulled into a service station, a young man approached—he was wearing a bandana, had a bucket in his hand and started washing my front window. My first reaction was not very spiritual. I was about to tell him to go away when the Holy Spirit intervened.

Praying that Daniel and Madison would behave, I leapt out of the car and approached the disheveled window washer. "Excuse me, but God told me that you have just gotten out of jail," I explained. "When you were a young boy, you were called of God to preach the gospel and you have been running from the call. You need to go back home and preach the gospel!"

Instantly, the window washer dropped his bucket and rag, turned and started to flee. I figured he simply thought that I was a lunatic. Because the message had been from God, I yelled after him, "Wait a minute, where are you going!" He turned back and said, "Lady, you are right, I just got out of prison. I was called of God to preach in my grand-father's church and I have been running from God for years. I am going back home to tell everyone what happened and I am going to preach the gospel."

What happened? One moment I was a normal everyday woman having her gas tank filled, the next moment something paranormal was happening.[1] What happened at that gas station is called prophetic evangelism and it is just one way in which God's ordinary people live supernatural lives.

You Can Tap Into the Power

Many Christians see very little, if any, of God's supernatural power. Others regularly see it manifest in their lives. What sets apart those who see the power from those who do not? While God has worked in many ways through many different people, most often people who live supernatural lives have had what can be called an Acts 1:8 experience with the Holy Spirit. This occurrence doesn't happen like some late-night movie in which an alien comes and snatches bodies. People who see the power of the Holy Spirit in their lives aren't invaded; rather, their change comes through an invitation—an invitation they give to the Holy Spirit. The Holy Spirit is the person of the Godhead (God the Father, God the Son, and God the Holy Spirit) who is in charge of the supernatural here in the earthly realm. All you need to do is ask, and He will come.

Often people who live supernatural lives have had what can be called an Acts 1:8 experience with the Holy Spirit.

After the disciples believed in Christ and were born again, the Lord told them that He was going to send them the Holy Spirit. This experience—that some call being baptized in the Holy Spirit and others call receiving the fullness of the Holy Spirit—completely changed their lives. Jesus encouraged them to be transformed:

But you shall receive *power* when the Holy Spirit has come upon you; and you shall be witnesses to me in Jerusalem, and in all Judea and Samaria, and to the end of earth (Acts 1:8, emphasis added).

The Holy Spirit Changed My Life

It takes an encounter with the Holy Spirit to receive the power to do what God wants you to accomplish in your life. I had this kind of experience in 1972, while I was in college. At one point I had moved home, then back to college and I was anxious about my scholarship coming through. The circumstances of my life started to pile up and I began to have feelings of depression. At times, my hands shook so much that it was difficult for me to play the piano. Each day I would force myself to sit down to practice, but I had to work at it to steady my hands on the keyboard. You can imagine the seriousness of this situation as I was earning a degree in music education.

One day a friend gave me a book that described the Holy Spirit. I knew that the Holy Spirit was God, but I was not intimately acquainted with Him. I also had heard about what I thought were weird practices, such as speaking in tongues, laying hands on the sick, and falling on the floor. To my recall, I had only met one or two people who claimed that they actually spoke in tongues.

I Had Questions for God

The book explained that it was important to invite the Holy Spirit to take complete control in your life, and it described speaking in tongues. For me, this was all very deep water. Nonetheless, I reasoned, *What could it hurt for me to ask God about this?*

I dug deeper by reading the book of Acts. This verse leapt off the page:

But you shall receive power when the Holy Spirit has come upon you; and you shall be witnesses to Me in Jerusalem, and in all Judea and Samaria, and to the end of the earth (Acts 1:8).

The time finally came when I felt that I was as ready as I would ever be to have a serious talk with God about the Holy Spirit. While I had many questions, I specifically wanted to know about speaking in tongues. Frankly, I was scared of that. I had heard many bizarre stories about people who rolled on the floor and acted very strange.

At last, my desperation overrode my fears. Sitting cross-legged on the floor, I started to pray, "Dear God, there isn't any gift that You have for me that I don't want. So, if You want to give me more of the power of the Holy Spirit and the gift of tongues, I want to receive them." For a few moments, nothing happened—then all of a sudden it was as if God opened up heaven and poured peace into every part of me. I had never seen anyone lift up his or her hands in the air to worship God; nonetheless, I did. It seemed natural, even an expression of thanksgiving.

I basked in this peace for as long as I could, but I needed to take a bath and leave for something at school. I've heard many people tell about how God speaks to them in the shower. That was exactly what happened with me! I started to sing—only it wasn't like any singing I had ever done, and it wasn't in English!

Wow, I thought, *this is amazing!* I had never sung so beautifully. In fact, it seemed more heavenly than anything I could have made with my own earthly style—with or without voice lessons! I had been told that if you sang about the blood of the Lamb, the song had to be coming from God. The devil cannot initiate such a song. Knowing this, I was excited that the first lyrics out of my mouth were, "Are you washed in the blood of the lamb?" I sang all of the verses, and I did it in a language that sounded like German.

> The incredible peace continued to wash over my soul. The depression was lifted, and joy took its place.

Next I sang, "When I survey the old rugged cross." I was having a wonderful time! When I finished the second song, I pondered, *Can I sing all those verses again in the same way?* By that point I was singing in a different language. It sounded like French. Though I did not know all of the languages, as I continued my singing, I am sure that I sang not only in German and French, but in other languages as well.

The incredible peace continued to wash over my soul. The depression was lifted, and joy took its place. Without an adequate vocabulary to describe what was happening to me, I just kept repeating, *Wow! Wow! Wow!*

God Answered by Changing Me

My next thought was, *I wonder if I can speak in tongues?* Singing in various languages was great, but I wanted to speak in a heavenly language. With that, beautiful words poured out of my mouth. I wasn't out of control; rather, I seemed completely in tune with God—more than I had ever been in my life. "Lord," I requested, "I want to know what I'm saying." At that moment, English words filled with praises to God poured into my mind.

How did this experience change me? For one, the Scripture simply came alive. I wondered, *Look at these verses in the Bible! Where have they been hiding?* There was so much that I had never seen in my 15 years as a Christian. (I accepted the Lord into my life at 5 and was 20 at the time of this experience.)

The next difference I noticed was that I became bolder in my witnessing. I indeed received power to witness when the Holy Spirit came upon me. That's not all. Moreover, I had an incredible sense that I was a supernatural creation of God. Suddenly I knew information about people that I could never have known on my own. I now know that this is one of the gifts of the Holy Spirit and it is called the word of knowledge.

Not only did I realize that God had changed me, but others noticed, too. My classmates would walk up to me and say, "It happened to you, didn't it?"

"What happened to me?" I would query.

"You know," they'd say. "You received the power of the Holy Spirit."

Of course, they were right. I was totally and radically changed.

I had become "one of them." I began walking around supernaturally natural. In the beginning, I wasn't sure how to cooperate with what had occurred in my life when I invited the Holy Spirit in with all His fullness. One thing I was certain, however, was that I was radically changed.

Naturally, I Moved Forward in the Supernatural

Initially I didn't know that there was so much more to this walking in the Spirit than I had previously realized. I remember telling a friend,

"I think this is something just for my private devotional time. I don't think that I will ever speak in tongues in front of anyone else." Little did I know that not only would I speak in tongues in public, but I would interpret what I was saying as well! (See 1 Cor. 12:10).

At the time of this supernatural experience, I wasn't yet married. Mike and I got married in August 1973. At the time, he hadn't yet had this kind of visitation. However, he was not opposed to it. In fact, sometimes when we would kneel down to pray I would pray in tongues and he would respectfully wait. It's not that I would pray very long. I was a novice to all of this and I was still in my I-don't-think-that-I-will-ever-speak-in-tongues-publicly stage.

After a few years, I became a bit frustrated, wanting Mike to walk more in the supernatural realm. Pushing him, trying to manipulate him to be more deeply spiritual than he was, availed nothing. At last I did what I should have done all along: I allowed the Holy Spirit to do His supernatural work in Mike's life.

Mike Joins the Journey

One day Mike came home from work with an audiocassette recording of what we call singing in the Spirit. This way of worshiping God was new to me. In my initial experience with the Holy Spirit, I had not heard corporate worship that included the use of a spiritual language.

I'll never forget the two of us with our ears glued to an old portable tape player. The audio was scratchy, but the sound was heavenly! The presence of God filled our little apartment to such a degree that Mike and I clung to each other and cried. We were both getting more and more hungry for more of the supernatural in our lives.

God continued to work sweetly with us. Mike wasn't resistant to the Holy Spirit—it was just so new to think about being intimate with Him.

For a long time, Mike had been trying to get a job in management. At last his big break came and he switched jobs. God was moving through this repositioning because the secretary for his new group was one of those supernatural beings. She was African-American and invited us to her church, Crenshaw Christian Center.

We Go to "One of Those Churches"

I almost hate to admit that we were both excited and a bit scared to go to "one of those churches." My recall is that I had decided that I would go, but if anyone did anything too weird, I was out of there—even if I had to make a door through the back wall where there was no door!

The service was amazing! It was fascinating being almost the only Caucasians—and it was quite good for us. Mike and I were so thrilled that we also went to the Sunday evening service to further check things out. Being in a room full of the supernatural presence of God was electric. One of the most exhilarating parts of the service was the testimonies of people who had been healed. A woman stood up and shared how she had been eaten up with cancer, but now she was totally free of the disease. Another person had suffered from a severely crooked back, but it was now straight. Wow (the word I seem to use when the Holy Spirit is moving), this stuff was real! We could hardly sleep that night because of our excitement over what we had seen.

The following Sunday, Mike and I were earnestly seeking God's direction for our lives. Was the Lord leading us to join this church? We were astounded in the evening service as someone spoke in tongues, and another person interpreted. The prophecy was "When the invitation comes, you are to join the church. Follow me and let the spiritually dead bury the dead." We understood. The church we had attended was full of wonderful people, but they didn't believe that healing was for today, nor did they seek after any of the other gifts that we were hungry to experience. Needless to say, when the invitation was given, we practically ran to the front of the church.

Mike Encounters the Holy Spirit

Mike went to a small room because he wanted to be prayed for to receive the fullness of the Holy Spirit and to speak in tongues. I paced the floor, holding our daughter who was just a baby at the time. I almost pounced on him when he came out. "What happened, what happened?" I questioned. He was kind of quiet and said, "I was prayed for, but I didn't speak in tongues."

You have to understand my husband to know how hard it was for him to give himself to speaking in tongues.

You have to understand my husband to know how hard it was for him to give himself to speaking in tongues. I used to call him Mr. Spock after the television character that was very cerebral. Despite Mike's unyieldingness, the Holy Spirit wasn't finished with him. A few nights later he was rocking the baby to sleep and he started to sing—only he wasn't singing in English! It is fascinating to note that he received speaking in tongues in song, just like I did!

Was he changed? I would say so. He became very hungry for the things of God. Each Sunday he would drag me to church. He would pray for people and share the love of God with them. Now both of us were supernaturally natural.

What Are the Signs of a Supernatural Life?

Becoming supernaturally natural doesn't make you weird, as I thought it would. On the contrary! Rather than acting like you are from the moon, you walk around with the power of the Holy Spirit and do what comes naturally, only from the perspective of the heavenly realm. When you flow in this manner, even unbelievers will be awed by the amazing power of God. Even though their heads might not truly understand what is happening, their hearts will attest that God is at work.

My life as a supernatural creation has been vastly fulfilling. Actually, having a Pentecost experience like the ones recounted in the book of Acts makes us normal in the spiritual realm. God should be able to use all of us as He heals the sick, casts out demons and reveals words of knowledge. The rest of this book takes you on a supernatural adventure. As you read you will see how to walk in the power of the Holy Spirit.

Keep the Faith, the Gifts Will Come
I am aware that there are some who may have asked God for the gift of tongues or the baptism of the Holy Spirit, yet might not have seen any

change. Please do not be discouraged. If you asked for the Holy Spirit to come in, He did!

> If a son asks for bread from any father among you, will he give him a stone? Or if he asks for a fish, will he give him a serpent instead of a fish? Or if he asks for an egg, will he offer him a scorpion? If you then, being evil, know how to give good gifts to your children, how much more will your heavenly Father give the Holy Spirit to those who ask him! (Luke 11:11-13).

I know some believers who have asked for the fullness of the Spirit but do not speak in tongues—they are some of the most Spirit-filled people I know! They still manifest the fruit of a supernatural life.

You Will Receive Power

I have already quoted Acts 1:8, but it is worth citing again: "But you shall receive power when the Holy Spirit has come upon you." This is an important truth to grasp because I believe that one significant evidence of the fullness of the Holy Spirit is power.

Peter Wagner, in his commentary on the book of Acts, wrote about the apostle Peter being filled with the Holy Spirit on the Day of Pentecost:

> This is not a mere reiteration of the theological fact that all true Christian believers are indwelt by the Holy Spirit. At conversion, we are all "made to drink into one Spirit" (1 Cor. 12:13). Paul also says, "The Spirit of Him who raised Jesus from the dead

dwells in you" (Rom. 8:11). However, being "filled with the Spirit" is a special empowering of the Holy Spirit over and above the ordinary, something that God desires and that we as individuals are actively to pursue.[2]

Jack Hayford, who is one of the most balanced leaders of our time, has written a book titled *The Beauty of Spiritual Language*. This is an excellent study for anyone who seeks an experience with the Holy Spirit. In it Hayford discusses the Pentecostal belief that speaking in tongues is the initial evidence of the Spirit's baptism.

As readily as I want to honor my Pentecostal forbearers for preserving the testimony of tongues and for generating a passion for Spirit-fullness among millions, at the same time I confess that I believe an unintended but nonetheless restrictive barrier was built. . . . I am referring to a classical Pentecostal conviction: the historic tradition that requires tongues as "the evidence," verifying the validity of a person's being baptized in the Spirit.[3]

Hayford lists signs of the Holy Spirit's fullness.

"What is the Bible's sign of Holy Spirit fullness?" With regard to signs of the Holy Spirit's fullness, everyone acknowledges that

1. *Love* is the first and foremost we should expect.
2. Next, few would challenge the proposal that if love is first, surely power must be the second sign we would anticipate.

3. A third arena of expectation may be found in the entire list of "signs" in 1 Corinthians 12:8-10. The nine gifts listed there are revealed as the unique domain of the Holy Spirit Himself. Additionally, the full complement of the nine fruits listed in Galatians 5:22-23 are reasonable expectations to be manifested as traits of His character working in us.[4]

What is important is that each of us invites the Holy Spirit into our lives. Claudio Freidzon, a leading Argentine Christian who travels around the world ministering on the subject of the Holy Spirit, has written a wonderful book titled *Holy Spirit, I Hunger For You.* His story makes the point:

The year 1992 represented a new period in my ministry. God poured out a saltshaker on my tongue, causing an intense spiritual thirst—a hunger for the Holy Spirit! He not only filled my cup with the Holy Spirit but He made the Spirit overflow toward others.[5]

There Will Be a Great Hunger

Perhaps, like Claudio Freidzon, you have become hungry for the Holy Spirit and His fullness. I believe that we are on the verge of seeing a vast number of people being swept into the kingdom of God and receiving the Holy Spirit—much like what happened in the late 1960s and throughout the 1970s. We will experience a great outpouring of miracles from ordinary, supernaturally natural believers who have invited an invasion of the Holy Spirit into every aspect of their lives.

Here is an explanation that I like to give that explains the difference between being born again and that of being born again *and* filled with the Holy Spirit:

When you get born again, it is like a coke bottle that has been thrown into a lake. The bottle is in the lake. However, when you are baptized in the Holy Spirit, it is like the coke bottle is completely filled with the water and you are immersed in the lake. The lake water is now not only around you but also in you.

We are on the verge of seeing a vast number of people being swept into the kingdom of God—much like what happened in the late 1960s and throughout the 1970s.

If you are not already walking as a supernaturally natural creation of God, you can become so right now at the beginning of this book. Are you a believer in Jesus? Have you ever invited Him to be your Savior? While this book is not primarily about how to become a Christian, being a Christian is primarily about living the supernatural life. If you have never taken this first, most important step, you can take it right now. Just say the following prayer, or one like it using your own words.

*Dear Jesus, I recognize myself as a sinner in need of forgiveness.
I see that You are the only way, and from this day forward I want
You as the redeemer of my life. Forgive me, restore me and lead
me in a new way—Your way. Thank You.*

Most of you reading this book said the above prayer, or one similar to it, a long time ago and you have seen the difference Jesus makes in your life. Now you want to have more power. Just say the next prayer, or one similar to it in your own words.

*Father God, right now I ask You to baptize me in the Holy Spirit.
I want to be filled to overflowing.*

It really is this simple. Since there is nothing that God has for you that you don't want, ask Him to enable you to speak in tongues.

1. First ask (see Luke 11:13).
2. Believe that you have received.
3. Ask the Lord to give you a new language to praise Him.
4. Open your mouth to speak. The language will not come through your natural process. This happens so that you won't think in English, or whatever language you speak, and then interpret accordingly. Rather, it will come out in tongues.
5. Don't be discouraged if you do not speak in tongues at that moment. If you have asked for the Holy Spirit and given Him an invitation to come into your life and fill you completely, He has done what you have asked.

6. It is important to repent if you have ever said that speaking in tongues was not for today because that can create a blockage. Also, it sometimes helps to break generational curses off your life. (For help in this area, see my chapter on breaking curses in *Deliver Us from Evil*.[6])

7. As you are praying in the Spirit, write down the thoughts that come to you during that time and expect God to speak new things to you.

Don't be surprised if you start speaking in a beautiful language. You might even sing as Mike and I did. Some people initially only receive a few words, and, for others, complete sentences pour out.

Remember that you have now received power because you have asked the Holy Spirit to come in and fill you to overflowing. Start your journaling at the end of this chapter by recording the date and experience that you had with the Holy Spirit.

Are You Ready to Start Your Supernatural Adventure?

One key to walking in the supernatural is not only to receive the empowering of the Holy Spirit but also to maintain your relationship with Him by receiving fresh touches from Him daily.

Ephesians 5:18-20 gives you more insight on how to do this:

And do not be drunk with wine, in which is dissipation; but be filled with the Spirit, speaking to one another in psalms and hymns and spiritual songs, singing and making melody in your heart to the Lord, giving thanks always for all things to God the Father in the name of our Lord Jesus Christ.

While there is an initial baptism, it is important to receive fillings of the Holy Spirit on a daily basis.

Peter Wagner underscores the need:

I make a habit daily of asking God to fill me with His Holy Spirit, and I believe He does, because Jesus said that just as a good father will not give a scorpion to a son who asks for an egg, "How much more will your heavenly Father give the Holy Spirit to those who ask Him!" (Luke 11:13).[7]

If you have spoken in tongues in the past, why don't you take some time in prayer right now? Speaking in tongues edifies you (see 1 Cor. 14:4). It spiritually charges your batteries. After you have prayed in tongues a little while, take time to be still and listen to what you are hearing from God in your spirit. Then, take time to write it down in the journaling section that follows this chapter.

Your Holy Spirit Adventures

Have you been baptized in the Holy Spirit? If so, recount your experience and not when it happened. How did this change your relationship with God? If not, have you asked God for the baptism? What is keeping you from asking right now?

Have you spoken in tongues? Recount your first experience with a new heavenly language. If you have never spoken in tongues, have you asked God for this gift? What is keeping you from asking for it right now? (Note: Remember, this is a journal, not a test. Be honest and open about your experience and allow God to grow you in the supernatural!)

PLUGGED INTO THE SUPERNATURAL

After receiving the power of the Holy Spirit, my life changed a lot. Each day was a new adventure with God. I couldn't wait to wake up and see what He would do in my life!

I Dive into Deeper Water

As I already noted, one of the most wonderful differences I noticed was that the Scriptures would simply come alive. It seemed that on every page there was something new to discover. First Corinthians 14:39 was one of those "new" verses:

> Therefore, brethren, desire earnestly to prophesy, and *do not forbid speaking in tongues* (emphasis added).

Other Scriptures leapt out as well. At times, the Holy Spirit would give me a revelation that I didn't realize was something from Scripture. I would run home and open my Bible to see if God had anything to say about that particular subject. One such revelation concerned laying hands on people for physical healing and to release the power of God.

I once told a friend, "I have this feeling that one day I'm going to put my hands on people and they are going to be healed!" Some of you may be thinking, *So what? Doesn't the Bible talk about that?* You are right, it does—but at that time in my life I didn't really know what the Bible taught about healing.

After a little personal epiphany, I decided to study about the laying on of hands for healing. As I devoured verse after verse, one passage stuck out:

And these signs will follow those who believe: In My name they will cast out demons; they will speak with new tongues; they will take up serpents; and if they drink anything deadly, it will by no means hurt them, *they will lay hands on the sick, and they will recover* (Mark 16:17-18, emphasis added).

The part of the Scripture in italics grabbed my attention. I knew that I spoke in tongues and that I wasn't ready to think about picking up snakes or drinking poison, but the laying of hands on the sick intrigued me. I had already had the revelation that healing power would come out of my hands, but I didn't know how that worked.

After a little personal epiphany, I decided to study about the laying on of hands for healing.

This all happened toward the beginning of my journey into understanding the power of the Holy Spirit, which has continued for many years. In this chapter, I am just laying out some of the process. As I noted in chapter 1, one big event that helped move my husband, Mike, and me along was finding and joining a group of Christians who believed that healing was for today. The people at the church we joined in Los Angeles really believed that they could and would do miracles!

Some People Think I Am Crazy
Some of the people at our former church thought that we were crazy. I learned that when I tried to tell them about the Holy Spirit. Thinking

that everyone I knew would be excited about my discoveries, I was astounded to find that some thought that I had dived into the deep end of the swimming pool. A few of them probably figured that I had hit my head on the bottom of the pool as well!

I received a couple of responses like, "Cindy, don't say things about laying hands on people. That all passed away. People already think that you are from the moon and this is certainly not going to help." Actually, they didn't understand that by embracing the spiritual realm in my life, I had, in a matter of speaking, gone far, far beyond the moon!

I Stood in a Prayer Line

As happens at many churches, at the end of each service ours would invite people to come forward for prayer. During my searching time, I went forward for prayer. I was going through a massive paradigm shift. There I was, working on my master of arts in teaching music, Mrs. Educated Person, standing in a long line of people waiting for this pastor I hardly knew to lay hands on me.

It is important to add that I did need a physical healing. I had some female troubles and went forward asking for a miracle. It seems that there was one hitch for me in all of this. As I carefully watched this line-thing, I came to understand that the people who were receiving prayer were also falling over onto the carpet!

I tried to analyze the situation. Was the pastor pushing them over? Was it mass hypnosis? No matter the cause, I resolved that I was not going to act stupid like those other people. When the time came, I was going to get my healing, thank you very much, then turn around and walk away—at least that was my plan.

When God is teaching you to walk as a supernatural creation, it seems like many of your plans turn out very different from what you had hoped. As I stood in the line, the pastor headed my way. The choir sang "Rise and Be Healed in the Name of Jesus" and my heart thumped like a big bass drum. Before I knew it, it had happened! I didn't understand how such a thing could have occurred, but suddenly I felt like I was floating to the floor. To my recall, I didn't even see the pastor near me or hear his prayer.

The wonderful thing was that I felt great! I had been healed of my sickness. The weird thing was that after I left, I convinced myself that the falling-to-the-floor thing was totally psychosomatic.

I Resisted Falling Down

Mike and I kept attending, soaking up new teachings on healing. Later I was suffering from bad headaches and decided to get in that healing line again. However, this time I knew that I could resist whatever happened to make me fall backward onto the floor. At least, that was my plan.

I couldn't believe what happened when I got to the front of the line! Preparing myself not to fall, I planted my feet firmly on the floor and sucked in my breath. The pastor was approaching me. All of a sudden that same sense of my body falling onto the sanctuary's nice, thick carpet overwhelmed me again!

This time I knew that I knew that the pastor did not push me. Wow! (There is my favorite word again.) This falling-under-the-power thing was real. What's more, my headache was gone, gone, gone!

My friend Carlos Annacondia describes falling under the power of the Holy Spirit as a wonder. This falling down did happen when Jesus was in the garden.

Jesus, therefore, knowing all things that would come upon Him, went forward and said to them, "Whom are you seeking?" They answered Him, "Jesus of Nazareth." And Judas, who betrayed Him, also stood with them. Now when He said to them, "I am He," they drew back and fell to the ground (John 18:4-6).

I don't know about you, but I'd like an instant replay of Judas being blasted to the ground!

This falling-under-the-power thing was real. What's more, my headache was gone, gone, gone!

After spending time on the church carpet for a second time, I knew that healing was for today. It was not just a theological theory, but I had actually been healed. The next step was for me to lay hands on the sick and see them healed, too.

I Become a Guinea Pig

I have to admit that this was a scary step. First of all, I had to find someone who would *let me* lay hands on them. That could be a problem as I hadn't made any new friends in the church we had joined, and my old friends were in their Cindy-is-from-the-moon stage. At last I knew that there was only one solution. I looked down at my hands and surmised,

I have hands, and I have a body. If the power of God comes out of these hands for healing, and who knows what else, then I can be the guinea pig for this experiment!

While preparing myself for this very personal prayer time, I read Bible verses that noted hands. One stopped me in my tracks.

His [God's] brightness was like the light; He had rays flashing from His hand, And there His power was hidden (Hab. 3:4).

I put two and two together. I am made in the image of God. Since this is true, I must also have rays or power that could come from my hands. Wow! That is why you use your hands, and not your elbow, or some other part of your body to lay hands on the sick.

Feeling totally equipped, I pondered as to where I should conduct the great experiment. Our first little house had lots of windows, but I needed a private place. The bathroom! Of course, that was the room where I had received my supernatural infilling, and it had no windows!

Carefully I picked up my Bible, went into our very tiny bathroom and closed the door behind me. Quietly I stood still and meditated on what I had learned over the previous few weeks about being a supernatural creation. Another Scripture popped into my mind:

He who believes in Me, as the Scripture has said, out of his heart will flow rivers of living water (John 7:38).

The *King James Version* translates this as "out of his belly will flow rivers of living water."

From John 7:38, I deduced that my heart or belly must be the generator plant of the Holy Spirit and that the power needed to get from my belly to my hand. If this was true, then I needed to release the power so that it could flow out of my belly, through my arm and then out of my hand. Because I was both dispersing and receiving the power, the actual laying on of hands (or hand, as I used just one) had to plug me into the power that was flowing.

Is this going to work? I asked myself. *Well, no one will know what has happened here but God and me; so here goes the great experiment!*

First I put my hand on my belly and said out loud, "All right, I'm releasing the power of God right now to start leaving my belly." Strangely enough, I could feel something happen inside of me. It's hard to describe, but it was warm and electric.

"Next," I said, still talking out loud, "I release this power to flow into and down my arm."

By this time I definitely could feel that the air in that tiny space seemed charged with God's power. I waited a moment for the power to get down my arm. "Lastly," I said, "I release the anointing out of my hand and plug myself into it."

With this, I reached my hand up and put it on my forehead. In the next moment I flew through the air and found myself *in the bathtub!* (There really wasn't any other place to go in the small room!)

I sat there a moment, simply stunned at what had transpired. Then I said, you guessed it, "Wow, God, that was awesome! I wonder if I could do that again!"

Something beyond anything that I had ever dreamed in my life took place in that little bathroom. I had so many paradigm shifts that I was stripping my gears! "God's power is real, real, real!" I shouted, and then thought, *This is amazing, simply amazing!*

Let's Do It Again!

Standing to my feet—albeit a trifle on the wobbly side—I went through the same process again, only faster. "OK," I said in a strong, confident voice. "I am releasing the power of God from by belly. It's going into my arm and out of my hand. I'm placing my hand on my forehead . . ." BAM! This time I was draped across the bathtub rather than inside it.

I sat there, feeling simply glorious. After a few moments, I jumped up and ran out of the bathroom. I was laughing, laughing, laughing! I zipped around our little house (all 754 square feet of it) giggling. "The power of God works through me!" I preached to myself. "I'm just a little mother, with a small baby, who can teach music and is married to a great guy; but I'm supernaturally endowed with the anointing of God!"

From that day on I was eager to find people other than myself who would let me pray for them with the laying on of hands.

It's Elementary, My Dear Jacobs

The sad side about this leg of the adventure is that I was just discovering one of the foundational doctrines of the Christian faith: laying hands on the sick. I have found that many Christians, perhaps even you, likewise know little about this biblical practice.

Hebrews 6:1-2 sets the stage:

> Therefore, leaving the discussion of the elementary principles of Christ, let us go on to perfection, not laying again the foundation of repentance from dead works, and of faith toward God, of the doctrine of baptisms, of laying on of hands, of resurrection of the dead, and of eternal judgment.

I earnestly believe that practice makes perfect. Therefore, after learning that what I was doing was part of the *elementary* principles of Christianity, I decided that I needed to go to elementary school in my beliefs. I needed to do the first things first!

My mother came to visit. She loves me and thinks that I'm great. Her foot was hurting her, so I told her what I was learning about healing. I was so excited when she actually let me pray for her foot. The most wondrous part was that it got better!

Before long I'd lay hands on anything I could. Mike and I started praying for each other if we felt sick. We prayed for our baby, too, and we all started walking in health.

No One Was Being Healed. Why?

I also asked my friends to let their crazy, from-the-moon friend pray for them. Sad to report, few of them, if any, got healed. In fact, one day one of those people said to me, "Cindy, no one that you are praying for is getting healed."

That was really depressing to hear. I went back to the Manufacturer's handbook, the Bible. I reread Mark 16:18:

They will lay hands on the sick, and they will recover.

I decided that my part was to lay my hands on the sick. It was God's part to heal them. From that day on, I didn't let anything deter me—and I started seeing quite a few people healed. Some got better immediately, and others took time to recover.

My Challenge to You

I want to challenge you to include the laying on of hands in every part of your life. You don't have to have a huge measure of faith to begin. Simply do it because it is in the Bible, and God said to do it!

My part was to lay my hands on the sick. It was God's part to heal them.

The practice of laying hands on the sick may at first seem strange, but let me encourage you to cultivate it. As you pray for others, you will grow in your faith and knowledge that God wants to do miracles through you. As you start, keep notes about what you experience. Use the journaling page at the end of this chapter.

Peter Wagner Learns About Laying On of Hands
Dr. Peter Wagner, my spiritual mentor, told me an amazing story of when he first started praying for the sick. Some of you may have heard about Peter's class at Fuller Theological Seminary. He invited the late John Wimber, long-time leader of Vineyard Ministries International, to teach on healing. At that time, Peter, a good Congregationalist, had not seen many healings, nor had he actually prayed for people to *be* healed.

Wimber challenged Wagner in the area of laying hands on the sick. (I include this story to back up my point that you don't necessarily have to *feel* very spiritual or full of faith when you pray—you just need to obey God's Word.)

Before I tell this story, I want to relate to you a point that you may have already discovered if you have prayed for many people. Sometimes

God starts you with the hardest cases! In fact, there are hard cases and then there are *the hardest cases*—ones that require what I call creative miracles would fall into the second category.

Peter Wagner was teaching at Fuller in February 1987. It was during this time that he had a massive paradigm shift concerning healing. He was challenged, not only by Wimber, but also by his Argentine friend, Carlos Anacondia, to pray for the sick for creative miracles.

One day the son and daughter-in-law of the School of World Mission's dean, Paul Pierson, came to his office for prayer for their son. Steve and Sara Pierson had adopted a young child from Guatemala who was born with no ears. Here is Peter's own account:

> When he (the couple's child) came into my seminary office he had only a tiny nub on each side of his head with no ear canals. He also was partially blind in the left eye. It looked so hopeless that I confess that I had very little faith when I laid hands on his head and then his left eye and asked God to heal him in Jesus' name. There was no evidence of anything happening, so I tried to encourage Chris and his parents as much as I could and they left.
>
> About a half hour later when they were going into Marie Callender's restaurant, Sara said to Steve, "Do you see what I see?" He admitted that he had already seen it, but wasn't going to say anything. The ears had started to grow.
>
> The next morning they were driving down the street when Chris said, "Mommie, what does b-a-k-e-r-y spell?" Sara said, "You can't see that sign, you don't have your contact lens." But he did see it. He said, "Ever since Dr. Wagner prayed for my eye

it has been burning, and I can see better now."[1]

While Chris's ears did not grow out completely, God did create an ear canal and enough tissue that the doctors were able to surgically build him new ears. Why didn't God give him the complete supernatural healing? We don't know. However, we do know that God used the story to touch the medical community with His great power and might.

Let's Get Started

For some of you, this kind of supernatural experience concerning healing may be quite new. You might have prayed for the infilling of the Holy Spirit for the first time at the end of the last chapter. Let me encourage you to look at a few Scriptures concerning healing:

Surely He has borne our grief, and carried our sorrows; yet we esteemed Him stricken, Smitten by God, and afflicted. But He was wounded for our transgressions. He was bruised for our iniquities; the chastisement for our peace was upon Him. *And by His stripes we are healed* (Isa. 53:4-5, emphasis added).

Who Himself bore our sins in His own body on the tree, that we, having died to sins, might live for righteousness—*by whose stripes you are healed* (1 Pet. 2:24, emphasis added).

Bless the Lord, O my soul; And all that is within me, bless His Holy Name! Who forgives all your iniquities, *who heals all your diseases?* (Ps. 103:3, emphasis added).

Read these Scriptures and meditate on them. Reread Mark 16:18-20 and the book of Acts. Record your observations on the journaling page.

Many wondrous things happened in the Early Church, including miracles (read the entire book of Acts). If you are a believer, then you should expect God to heal the sick through you, too. After you study, put into practice what you've read. Find someone on whom you can lay your hands. It is important to walk as a supernatural creation of God. Whether or not you feel any power as you pray is not important. I have already noted this, but it is important enough to repeat: You need to simply obey in faith God's Word regarding healing.

It Is OK to Be a Fool for Christ
Some of you, no doubt, go to a church where the leaders do not believe that God can heal today. You may worry about what others will think of you if you offer to pray for someone who is sick. Remember that the apostles were willing to appear as "fools for Christ" (1 Cor. 4:10). Jack Deere, who started praying for the sick while on the staff of Dallas Theological Seminary, went through this same struggle.

> I went through this fear when I first began to pray for the sick. I wondered what my colleagues at seminary might think of me. I also wondered what my friends in the church would think of me. For many years I had taught them that God rarely, if ever healed through supernatural means in our time. What would they think of me if I began to pray for the sick, and people didn't get healed?[2]

Couldn't I Have Started with a Headache?
I recall an instance when I was first praying for the sick. Not long

after my bathroom experience with the laying on of hands, we moved to El Paso. I was sharing with a new friend of mine that God heals today. She looked at me and said, "Great, I know someone who is sick!"

I have to admit that I felt some trepidation. I felt even more anxious when she explained that she was a caretaker of a woman who had a stroke and, as a result, one of the woman's arms was shorter than the other. That really scared me. Inside I was praying and telling the Lord, *Father, I just moved here. Couldn't we start with a headache?* However, by that point I was in too deep to back out.

We walked into the room and I almost had faith failure when I looked at the woman. She looked like her next breath could be her last! *Oh no!* I thought and simultaneously panicked on the inside. *This is much, much worse that I thought!*

Quietly I approached the woman. I told her that I had come to pray for her and that God loved her. She just barely nodded her head at me, which I took as her saying, "Proceed." I raised both of her arms. They were paralyzed; but, indeed, one was shorter than the other.

I closed my eyes to pray, not because I thought it was a spiritual gesture, but because I didn't have enough faith to have my eyes open and say what I was going to say! Out of my mouth came the words, "I speak to you arm in the name of Jesus Christ—grow!"

I felt the arm move and surmised that the woman was trying to help me. That's when my friend started to shout, "It's growing! It's growing!" My eyes popped open! I couldn't believe it was happening even though I had been the one to pray! Sure enough, the arm was growing and became the same length as the other one. Hallelujah! The woman's health greatly improved after that as well.

From that day on I poured over books concerning the miraculous. I was on fire to be used more and more by God to heal the sick. Little did I know that one day I would pray for thousands at a time and before my eyes see the book of Acts happen on a regular basis.

You Can Pray, Too

Some of you may have learned about the laying on of hands years ago, and yet you rarely do so on a regular basis. If your friend or child has a headache, rather than offering to lay hands on then, you offer them an aspirin. Please consider going back to the elementary principles of the faith and believe God for a miracle first.

Writing about this time of my life has made me so happy. It's good to look back on the Holy Spirit adventures that one has had with God. Sometimes we need to remind ourselves of these times. It is kind of like recapturing your first love experience with the Holy Spirit. This might be the case with you as well. If so, I want to encourage you to sit with others and reminisce.

Whether you are just beginning to lay hands on the sick, or you have been doing it for many years, how about journaling your adventures in the place provided at the end of this chapter?

Your Holy Spirit Adventures

When was the first time you laid hands on someone and he or she was healed? Did God start you with a "tough" case, or an easy one? How did you feel when you heard of the person's miracle? Did it increase your faith?

When you prayed for the sick to be healed, what were the reactions of the people around you? Did they feel closer to God?

WHO'S WHO IN THE SPIRIT REALM?

If you were able to peel back the separation between the natural and supernatural dimensions and take a look, what would you see? First, you would notice that the supernatural, or spirit, realm is more full of spirit beings than you could ever imagine. You would see different orders of angels; you might even feel threatened or intimidated by various demons.

Of course, if you were to take a glimpse into heaven, you might possibly see things that you don't have human words to describe. Joy might fill your heart as you see loved ones who have gone on before you. It would thrill me to see what my dad and my grandmother do on a daily basis in heaven.

What Will a Look Inside the Spirit Realm Reveal?

The spirit, or supernatural, dimension that you would witness is more real than the natural one you presently call home. Why do I say this? I say it because the spirit realm is eternal and everlasting.

What does the "real" you look like? You might ask, "What do you mean, Cindy? I am the real me."

Yes, but what you see is the earthly suit of a spiritual being. If you stepped out of your body into eternity, you would be who you are going to be for the rest of forever. Many Christians believe, as I do, that you will look unique and be recognizable. I also believe that you will look the best you have ever looked! (This is good news for some of us older people.)

At the moment, the only way that you get snapshots of the spirit realm is through visions, dreams, spiritual discernment and supernatural knowledge. How do you know that what you see is really what is in the supernatural realm and not simply a product of our flesh? How do you know whether it is angelic or demonic? These are all valid and important questions. Let's explore them now.

You Need to Test the Spirits

The Lord knows that you will need answers to these questions because He warns you that you need to prove by Scripture the things that you experience spiritually. First Thessalonians 5:21 tells us to "Test all things; hold fast to what is good."

Heed the Biblical Warning

It is important for you to learn how to test all things because you also have a biblical warning about the end times.

> Now the Spirit expressly says that in latter times [and we are in those times now], some will depart from the faith, giving heed to deceiving spirits and doctrines of demons, speaking lies in hypocrisy, having their own conscience seared with a hot iron (1 Tim. 4:1-2, personal note added).

Our generation needs to be vigilantly on guard against deception and learn how to test the spirits because of the times we are in.

How do you learn to test what you think to be a supernatural experience? First of all, you need to be rooted and grounded in the Bible. The first thing that should pop into your head when you come into a supernatural situation is this: *Is this biblical?* In other words, can you find a place in the Bible where something like this happened?

These supernatural experiences can vary widely, and we will look at this in more detail on the next pages, but let me note that there are numerous biblical examples of angels interacting with human beings (for example, see Gen. 19:1; 32:1). There are also times when demons manifest themselves (for example, see Matt. 8:31; Mark 6:13). Satan himself talked to Jesus (see Matt. 4:10).

The first thing that should pop into your head when you come into a supernatural situation is this: "Is this biblical?"

Is the Spirit Angelic or Demonic?

I want to be careful how I explain this. Even though you find a biblical example of a particular supernatural experience, you still need to be able to discern *what spirit* (i.e., angelic or demonic spirits) may be interacting with you. This may sound a bit scary, but God has actually equipped you through the power of the Holy Spirit, as supernaturally natural beings, to test and deal with these kinds of experiences.

When you have a supernatural interaction with a spirit, if you still are not sure of the source, turn to others in the Body of Christ who operate by discerning of spirits. They can help you.

In his book *Your Spiritual Gifts Can Help Your Church Grow*, Peter Wagner gives this definition of the gift of discerning of spirits:

The gift of discerning of spirits is the special ability that God gives to some members of the Body of Christ to know with assurance whether certain behavior purposed to be of God is in reality divine, human or satanic.[1]

The divine, the human and the satanic (Satan's kingdom) are the three areas we will investigate.

Don't Go Overboard

Some people reject anything that is supernatural as being of the devil, while others purport to "discern" that there is a demon behind every bush. Roxanne Brant, in her book *How to Test: Prophecy, Preaching and Guidance*, recounts this story concerning a man who had definitely gone overboard in the area of supposedly seeing demons.

A man came to me and said that during that day and evening, in the past 12 hours, he had seen a total of 12 demons; one demon in the piano, two demons in his refrigerator, three in the pulpit and four in his living rooms, plus two more in his car. . . . Everywhere this man went, he saw demons. "What a vivid imagination you have," I told him, "and what a tremendous gift of suspicion also." The man said, "No, Rosanne, I am serious, God has given me the gift of the discerning of spirit and I see demons everywhere. In fact, several days ago, in a meeting filled with Christians, I saw one man who had 20 demons, another woman who had 35 demons, and another person who had 54 demons!"

I asked the gentleman how many *angels* he had seen that day as well, and he said to me, "I don't see angels, I just see demons."

I replied to him "Then you do not have the gift of discerning of spirits mentioned in 1 Corinthians 12:10. The reason I know this is that the gift Paul mentions here is a gift of "discerning of spirits," *not* "discerning of evil spirits."[2]

It is sad to note that people like this man make some others feel that this gift is not a real, legitimate one that operates in the Body of Christ today. The man in this story was deceived and gives those who have the real gift of discerning of spirits a bad name. It also hurts those who are called into the ministry of deliverance.

I agree with Peter Wagner, who observes that there are those with the true gift who can discern what is divine, what is human and what is satanic.

How Does Discernment Work?

People who have this gift see things in the spirit realm that others do not see. Small children who have this gift sometimes suffer because they will see things that may scare them—things that other children don't see. Two little ones may be resting in the same room. One will sleep like a baby while the other will cry because there is a monster in the room. What's the difference? It could be that the crying child has actually discerned a demonic presence in the room.

Daniel Learns to Rebuke the Enemy

Both of our children operate in discerning of spirits. They have done so since they were small children. They have seen demons and angels; at times they have an amazing ability to see into other people's hearts.

Years ago, when our son, Daniel, was 4, he was tormented by demonic visitations. The stuffed animals in his room seemingly would move on their own accord. There were other scary manifestations, too. At that time in our lives we didn't know much about praying through your house to get rid of demonic interferences.

I did, however, know that Daniel needed to learn to take authority over the enemy, so I taught him 2 Timothy 1:7: "God has not given me a spirit of fear, but of power, love, and a sound mind!" Knowing that Daniel was especially sensitive to the spirit realm because of his gift of discerning of spirits, I realized that the demonic realm would try to harass him if he didn't learn to rise up in his authority through the name of Jesus and rebuke the enemy.

The gift of the discernment of spirits functions as if you are wearing supernatural eyeglasses that enable you to peer into another dimension.

Each night before Daniel would go to sleep, we would quote 2 Timothy 1:7 together out loud. One pitch-black night Mike and I were awakened out of a sound sleep by Daniel shouting at the top of his voice: "Devil, in the Name of Jesus, I resist you. God has not given me a spirit of fear, but of power, love and a sound mind!"

After a few moments, Mike rolled over, looked at me and with a sleepy voice said, "Cindy, can't you teach him to do that quietly?"

Children are well able to learn to take their stand on Scripture just as adults do.

Put On Your Spiritual Eyeglasses

If you have the gift of the discernment of spirits, it functions as if you are wearing supernatural eyeglasses that enable you to peer into another dimension. While every believer can and should ask God for spiritual discernment, some will either be aware or actually see demons and angels more than others.

Do You Have the Gift?

How do you determine if you have this gift? First, you will have been aware of a realm that is largely unseen to many people. As a small child you were one of those who "saw" those things that went bump in the night. You may have exclaimed to your mother, "Oh, look at the pretty angels! Look, mommy, they're right there." Your mother, even if she also has this gift in operation, may or may not have seen the same thing.

What do I mean by seeing them? At times these spirit beings will almost seem as tangible as those with physical bodies. On other occasions, they will seem more shadowy but no less real.

Have you ever rounded the corner of your house and thought that you saw something out of the corner of your eye? Then the next thing that happened to you was that you felt something very unsettling that you couldn't quite put your finger on? Well, if it was a chill or dark feeling, that could have been a demonic presence in your house. Of course, angels could be present, too, but they generally would not produce trepidation. Those with discerning of spirits seem to have this happen to them every once in a while, but it will be a rare experience for others. I personally have found that the stronger the demons are in the geographic area I am in, the bolder they will be in their appearance.

I Knew That It Was Demonic

Some friends and I were in Vancouver, British Columbia, during the mid-1980s and were praying in preparation for a conference for women in ministry in that city. We had unknowingly booked a hotel room in the more questionable part of the downtown area. One day as I opened the door to get into a taxi, a man appeared right beside me. He was dressed completely in black, was Asian and had a white-painted face. The disturbing part of the whole picture was that he held two sharp hari-kari knives pointed right at my head! I glanced up and sensed that this was not of a natural origin and rebuked the spirit in the name of Jesus and told the spirit of death to leave, which it did.

We later found out that the area where we were was not only influenced by Asian occult but also had a high rate of violent crime and murder. Thank God for the discerning of spirits.

What could have happened to me if I had not discerned the origin of the spirit? While I realize it is speculation on my part, it is interesting to note that several women leaders who visited us had a terrible car accident on the way back to their city and one eventually died. In fact, we took a bus later that week to visit the survivors and lay hands on them in the intensive care unit of a hospital.

There are other times when you will see angels. I have a whole chapter on angels, so I will save that part for later.

What About the Human Factor?

Even though you have this gift, you need to be aware that your human-ness can get in the way of your discernment. Since each person is only one part of the Body and not the whole, you will never get to the place, even with the gift of discernment, where you don't, at times, need others to help process what you are "seeing" in the spirit. (In my case, I ask other Christians with the same gift to judge some of the things that I encounter in the supernatural realm.)

What can hinder your evaluation of what you may or may not be seeing? For one thing, fear.

Now, there are different kinds of fear. The fear of the Lord is the beginning of wisdom (see Prov. 1:7), but this fear is really a reverence for God based on an accurate understanding of God. There is also an abuse of the fear of the Lord; some people fear God because they have the idea that He is a vengeful, hating, monstrous bully who cares nothing for them. They fear God because they believe lies about God.

Fear can also be a legitimate emotional response to actual threats to safety or belongings. It is a fear based in reality. But fear can also be blown out of proportion due to inaccurate perceptions or an over-active imagination. This kind of fear is based on threats that are not real.

Then there's the fear caused by demonic spirits. This fear can be seeded with any kind of fear (real or imagined) and eventually gains a stranglehold on your emotions.

To understand this better you can apply Peter Wagner's divisions between the divine, the human and the satanic. The fear of the Lord is divine; the human fears are based in our real and perceived insecurities;

and demonic fear takes these fears, magnifies them, distorts them, and ultimately tries to turn them against God.

A demonic spirit of fear can make a person abnormally afraid of anything: for example, heights, confined spaces, the marketplace (going outside the home where there are other people). A demonic spirit of fear fools people into believing that demons (and Satan) are much more powerful than they actually are. If a demonic spirit of fear is not cast out, it can warp Christians, even Christians who have the gift of discernment of spirits!In fact, it can distort the actual discernment to the point of knowing there is a spirit, but not knowing if it is demonic or of God.

> A demonic spirit of fear fools people into believing that demons (and Satan) are much more powerful than they actually are.

There Is No Place for Fear

Many years ago we lived in Weatherford, Texas, in a lovely, tree-shaded neighborhood. One day I met a woman who lived a few houses away who told me that she could not even go the grocery store because she dreaded crowds. I said to her, "Why, that is nothing but a demon of fear!"

She was a nice Methodist woman who had never heard of such a thing, but she was quite desperate for help! I proceeded to quote 2 Timothy 1:7 to her (the same Scripture I gave to my son, Daniel).

For God has not given us a spirit of fear, but of power and of love and of a sound mind.

I asked this woman if she would like to be free of that spirit and she said, "Of course!" That was all I needed to know! Within moments she was totally free of that spirit's oppression and filled with the Holy Spirit. From that day forward she could go to the grocery store, or anywhere else that she wanted. Her agoraphobic condition has never returned.

Satan often tries to oppress those with the gift of discerning of spirits through a demonic oppression of fear. I was a very fearful child myself. Looking back, I now realize that this was generational, as my grandmother was also very fearful. One way that fear would manifest in my life was through a generational iniquity of worry.[3] In my Southern culture, we thought that if we loved someone then we also worried about them! However, what I felt went way past worry to fearful worry and anxiety. I renounced the iniquity of worry and broke it off of my life and have since been much more balanced in that area.

Wounded People Can Be Healed
Another open door that can color the effectiveness of discernment is woundedness. You may think that you discern someone's human spirit and that they are rejecting you, when in actuality what you detect is your own spirit of rejection or abandonment.

Because of this possibility, if you have the gift of discernment you need to make sure that you are free from unforgiveness, rejection, fear and other things that can impede your ability to discern. In this way, the gift will flow freely.[4]

People with a spirit of rejection will often unconsciously cause you to reject them. They have habit patterns that have been built into their life while growing up that sabotages their relationships.

You should ask the Lord to only see
what He wishes you to see.

People who cause damage in these areas may push others around and reject them on a daily basis by becoming controlling, manipulative or suffocating, while being totally unaware of what they are doing. Then when they are rejected, this spirit usually works in tandem with a spirit of abandonment that says, "See, nobody likes me. I knew that they wouldn't like me for very long anyway!" If you find that people are telling you over and over that you are controlling or needy, it never hurts to check to see if you really have a problem in these areas that you cannot see.

Demons Appear in Dreams
Those with the gift of discernment will find that demons will sometimes appear in their dreams as well. (Of course, this can happen to anyone.) If this is happening to you, you need to take authority in the name of Jesus and command the demons to stop visiting you in the night. You might need to pray over the room where you sleep, taking command over demonic interference.

Some young people with a prophetic gift, which often has a spirit of discernment attached, might be tormented by seeing way beyond what the Lord is trying to show them. You should ask the Lord to only see what He wishes you to see. Isaiah 42:19 makes this clear:

Who is blind but My servant, Or deaf as My messenger whom I send: Who is blind as he who is perfect, And blind as the Lord's servant.

You Should Refine What You See

While there are many things going on in the supernatural realm, you need to ask the Lord that you will only see those things that He wishes you to see. While the enemy may try to impose himself on your spiritual sight, you should not simply keep yourself wide open to view just any and everything in the spirit.

For those with this gift, why don't you pray this prayer with me?

Lord, I pray that I will not leave myself so wide open in the spirit realm that I see things that You are not wanting me to see.

After you pray that, pray a binding prayer against Satan's power:

I bind you, Satan, from tormenting me with visions that God does not want me to have. In the name of Jesus. Amen.

Another good prayer is one that cuts off any occult influence that you have through your forbears:

Father, I now renounce and break any occult involvement in my family back three or four generations. Forgive my family for their involvement and close any open door from the occult in my life. In Jesus' name. Amen.

The Power of a Curse Can Be Broken

One day a young man came to me after church and said, "Cindy, life is very hard on me because I can feel the witches cursing me from miles away. Anytime they send curses, they seem to hit me."

I replied, "George [not his real name], that is not right. For one, those curses should not be prospering against you unless you have some kind of open door [see Prov. 26:2]. You have left yourself wide open to them. Bind their power and shut the door to hyperspirituality." I also gave him the verse from Isaiah 42:19:

> Who is blind but My servant, Or deaf as My messenger whom I send? Who is blind as he who is perfect, And blind as the Lord's servant.

If you think that curses are coming against you, break their power but do not become obsessed with thinking about them.[5]

Can You Know Another Person's Spirit?

The final and quite significant function of discerning of spirits is the ability to supernaturally discern the human spirit of another person. If you have this gift, you will be able to tell your spouse things like "Honey, I don't know why, but you can't trust that person. Please don't get into business dealings with him."

Of course, Satan will try to assault the mind of the person receiving this information. He might try to tell them, "Your spouse is just being suspicious. So and so is a really nice person." Other emotions, such as jealousy, might also come into play.

I want to encourage you: Do not shrug off your feelings if you see a red flag being raised. After a few times experiencing these feelings, couples usually learn that they need to heed these cautions.

Everyone Can Discern in the Spirit Realm

Remember that I promised to let you know how to discern what is in the spirit realm even if you don't operate by the gift of discernment. First, realize that God wouldn't have told us to test all things if we could not do so! Second, look at these tips on how to test unusual occurrences that may be happening to you:

1. Is it biblical?
2. What is the fruit of what you are experiencing (i.e., does it bring you peace, make you afraid, confuse you)? God is not the author of confusion (see 1 Cor. 14:33).
3. Do others bear witness that what you thought you saw or felt was from God? If not, it might have been from Satan's kingdom. Keep in mind that your own flesh or heart desires can also get in the way of what you are seeing. (This is especially true when it comes to some kind of contact from those whom you loved who have died.)

The Gift of Discerning of Spirits Is a Gift from God
If you have the gift of discerning spirits, then you need to learn to use it correctly so that you can be a blessing to the Body of Christ. However, some people think that this gift is a curse rather than a blessing. As a

young college student, I grew tired of sensing so much in the spirit realm and didn't know how to accurately use my gift. One day I cried out to the Lord, "Turn it off, turn it off! I'm tired of feeling all of these things." I didn't know how to take what the Lord was showing me and pray through to a breakthrough for the people. Breakthrough is the true way to make the gift bring great change. The ability to do spiritual warfare and learn to resist the enemies' attacks against you and others is invaluable to the church.

However, at first the gift just scared me and I didn't know about the things I wrote in my first book, *Possessing the Gates of the Enemy*. After asking God to turn off the gift, He, for a season, did not allow me to flow in the gift of discernment. It felt as if I were blind! I suddenly realized that if that is how it feels for me not to be who God had meant me to be then I wanted the gift. I asked for it back, and He graciously gave it.

The gift of discerning of spirits is a wonderful gift that we need to recognize in the Body of Christ. I find that even though I operate in this gift myself, there are times when I need to be more discerning, and I am working on a regular basis to improve.

Your Holy Spirit Adventures

What is your understanding of discerning spirits? Have you ever sensed a supernatural spirit, either good or evil? Recount the experience and explain why it was vital to know from where the spirit came.

List some of your fears and identify which kind of fear it is. Do you harbor any unhealthy fear that keeps you from discerning the Spirit of God? Can you surrender that fear to God right now? Do you have any curses that need to be broken?

DOES DRY CLEANING HURT THE ANOINTING?

Through the years I have had some rather strange phone calls. I remember one in particular. At first I thought that it might be in the category of the call I received from a person who wanted me to raise her dog from the dead. However, I decided to hang on and listen to the woman before I came to a conclusion on whether the caller was legitimate.

Her first comment was, "Hello, I am calling from Scotland. Several years ago you prayed for a friend of mine in a conference in Dallas, Texas. At that time, as a gift, you gave her a lace collar that you had been wearing."

I had pretty much decided that this was a thank-you call. Indeed, it was, but not in the way I thought it would be! In a quiet and charming voice, the woman went on to say, "Cindy, my friend wanted me to phone and ask you if dry cleaning hurts the anointing?"

That got my full attention. I mumbled, "Excuse me, but could you please repeat that?" She again quite patiently restated the same question.

My brain was having a hard time relating the words "dry cleaning" and "anointing" in the same sentence! I decided that further explanation was in order to at least sort things out in my mind. She explained everything in great detail: "In 1984, my friend and I were at a conference where you were teaching women leaders in Dallas, Texas. At one point you prayed for my friend and the anointing of God was very heavy that day. As you finished, you took off your Battenberg lace collar and gave it to her as a gift. My friend realized that the collar was full of the anointing of God."

Remembering the Scripture that related healing to cloths taken from the body of the apostle Paul (see Acts 19:12), I listened with wonder. It seems that so many people had been healed by either touching or putting the collar on that it had gotten dirty. One particularly amazing story told of how the owner of the collar had been at work one day when a coworker mentioned that she was ill. "Wait right there!" said the lady. At that she ran home and took the collar out of her drawer and ran back to the office. "Go in the restroom and put this on!" She implored. As women often do, they went to the restroom together and the other lady went into one of the stalls, closed the door and put on the collar. A few moments later the owner of the collar heard a thud. The woman in the stall had fallen under the power [of the Holy Spirit] and later on got up completely healed! [Evidentially she did not hurt herself in the fall.]

After hearing this story I paused in a moment of stunned silence. Then I managed to stammer, "Ah, yes, well, to answer your question: No, I don't think that dry cleaning will hurt the anointing." After cheerfully thanking me, the sweet Scottish woman hung up the phone.

God Heals in Many Ways

The Bible is the Manufacturer's handbook, and it provides a number of different ways for people to be healed, including through prayer cloths. If one method doesn't seem to produce results, you can apply another. If you go to a hospital, a medical doctor might try more than one mode of healing. God works much the same way. While you can never put God in a box and think that you have figured out all of His incredible ways, it should not seem strange that there would be more than one way for Him to heal people.

God Heals Through Prayer Cloths (See Acts 19:12)

In my experience, the healings that came through the anointed lace collar aren't the only ones that have come through cloths. There have been other times when the anointing has been on a cloth that has been prayed over, or on an article of clothing worn by someone during a ministry time. For example, at the end of a healing conference in California, I felt that all of the speakers should anoint prayer cloths for everyone in the conference. We did so with amazing results.

> The laying on of hands is probably the most frequently used application of God's healing power.

One person testified that after the prayer cloth was laid on her, not only was an older woman who had been unable to sleep at night for some time healed, but many people in her neighborhood were healed as well.

You might consider these testimonies to be outlandish. However, there are many things that we see as being unusual only because we are not used to them. The proof of the matter is that anointed prayer cloths work! This is one way that God chooses to heal people today.

Let's look as some more of God's modes of healing.

God Heals Through the Laying On of Hands (See Mark 16:18)

The laying on of hands is probably the most frequently used application of God's healing power. Actually, if we understand that the Holy Spirit lives in us and is the power to heal through the name and atonement of

Jesus Christ, then this makes sense. As I demonstrated in my own account of laying hands on myself, when we lay our hands on a sick person, the power of the Holy Spirit goes through them and seeks out the sickness or disease to heal it. At times the person who prays may even feel warmth or a tingling in his or her hands. The power of the Holy Spirit can be likened to supernatural electricity. However, whether we feel anything or the person we are praying for feels anything is not relevant. It is our obedience to Scripture that counts.

There are many wondrous accounts of people who have been healed through the laying on of hands. For example, a friend of mine named Evelyn Hamon was healed. Evelyn is the wife of Dr. Bill Hamon, whom God has used to pioneer the personal prophecy movement. Bill and Evelyn head up Christian International, a ministry based in Santa Rosa Beach, Florida.

Evelyn battled with sugar diabetes for many years and had to take three different medicines to keep the disease under control. Not long ago she was dramatically healed. Here is her testimony:

For years I had sugar diabetes. A little over a week before I was healed I had a serious bout of insulin shock when I took my medicine and fell asleep without eating. When my husband came home, he was unable to rouse me. When the paramedics arrived my blood sugar level was in the 30s. It is supposed to be in a range of 80 to 120. This was a life-threatening situation and really scared my family.

Shortly after this incident, we had our annual Christian International conference. Pastor Guillermo Maldonado from Miami was ministering on healing in the evening service. At his request I brought my glucose meter to the meeting to take my glucose level right before he prayed for me. I did that right before he laid hands on me and I found it to be 309.

After the healing prayer, he requested that I take my level again. I did so and it had gone down a little over 100 points to 204. He laid hands on me a second time. This is biblical (see Mark 8:25). I tested my glucose levels again and they were down to 187.[1]

Evelyn's glucose levels have remained low, she no longer takes her medicine and she is completely healed. However, she does watch carefully what she eats.[2]

The icing on the cake is that her sister, Donna, who also had sugar diabetes was standing behind her that night when Pastor Maldonado laid hands on her. Donna had prayed, "Well, Lord, if you are going to heal my sister, heal me too!" And He did! This proves that you can't put God in a box in the way that He will heal. This was simply a response to Donna's faith as she cried out to the Lord even though hands were not laid on her.

Healing Will Come Through an Anointing with Oil (See Jas. 5:14-16)
Why does God heal through the application of oil? It is symbolic of the Holy Spirit. I have found that there are times when I have prayed for people who could not receive healing any other way, yet they received one when I anointed them with oil. Somehow the application of oil—just like you might dispense a salve as a medicine—causes faith to rise up for a miracle.

James 5:14-16 not only instructs Christians to have elders anoint the sick, but the passage also links healing with the need for forgiveness of sin. No matter the mode of healing, this connection is important to understand. Unforgiveness of sin can be a real hindrance to receiving your healing. I was once diagnosed with a grapefruit-sized tumor. Someone called me with a word of knowledge that if I found the root and removed it, I would be healed. *What could be the root?* I pondered. Finally the Lord showed me my hurt and unforgiveness against a pastor who had called me a false prophet. After I called some friends together and confessed my sin to them, they prayed for my healing.[3] Ten days later, when I returned to the doctor, the tumor was completely gone.

The application of oil can bring about a healing, but so can the removal of unforgiven sin.

You Can Stand in Faith to Recover (See Mark 16:18)

Sometimes you can receive prayer for healing but it will not obviously manifest right away. It may seem like the symptoms of the sickness are still there. When this happens to you, stand in faith that you indeed are recovering. Quote healing Scriptures and resist the enemies' attempts to convince you that you will never be healed.

A doctor will give you a prescription when you visit him at his office, but you have to go to a pharmacist to have that prescription filled. Once you get your medicine, you have to follow the instructions, which often means taking repeated doses over a period of time. No one in his or her right mind throws out medicine after taking the first pill. You keep taking it until you are well. Why should it be any different when you visit Doctor Jesus, the great physician, to receive His healing power? You receive your medicine through the laying on of hands or the anointing of oil, and then you follow up with regular applications of "medicine," which is the reading and claiming of Scripture.

I had to follow these steps after I confessed my sin and received healing prayer for the grapefruit-sized tumor. For ten days the pain seemed just as great and the enemy kept telling me, "You aren't healing. You are just deceiving yourself!" I resisted those words. I audibly proclaimed, "No, devil, you are wrong. I am healed by the stripes of Jesus!" In my life, it has been a pattern that others receive instantaneous healings particularly at times when I have to stand and fight for a healing of my own.

God Gives Words of Knowledge (See 1 Cor. 12:18)

While many people, such as Oral Roberts, have been used of God to see miracles occur, primarily through the laying on of hands, I personally have seen more miracles come through words of knowledge. What do I mean by words of knowledge?

> A word of knowledge is information given to you supernaturally by God that you could not have known except by revelation.

A word of knowledge is information given to you supernaturally by God that you could not have known except by revelation. I say *word* of knowledge because it is only a part of God's knowledge (see 1 Cor. 12:8). The use of this gift extends far beyond healing, but it is powerful when in a healing context. I often use the gift when ministering to large crowds in stadiums because it can reach the most people in the shortest amount of time.

At those moments when I am praying for the sick, I often say that I am simply a reporter for God. By this I mean that I am merely passing along what God wants to do at a particular time and in a particular place.

At a meeting in Resistencia, Argentina, a dramatic miracle occurred as I reported what God was about to do. That particular night, about 20,000 people filled an open field. It was rather wild: nearby Macumba witches cursed us as we openly burned occult items in a big oil drum. People placed certain objects in the fire and screamed out loud as demons fled.

During the meeting, we had intercessors located under the platform. When events would get too hot and we would seem to be losing ground, I would simply stomp on the platform to let the intercessors know "We need more prayer up here!" They would add more fuel to the prayer fires and the power of God would manifest in dramatic ways.

During the service, I received a word of knowledge from the Lord that there was someone present who could not walk—that this person should rise, be healed and try to walk. A few minutes later, in the midst of the crowd I could see a medical apparatus being passed until it arrived at the platform and was given to me. Moments later, a five-year-old child was lifted up and placed in front of me. I asked for the story of the child. We heard how her grandmother had brought her to the meeting. The little girl had been unable to walk and had worn the apparatus simply to stabilize her body.

That morning her grandmother had promised her that at the meeting "the man from Galilee" would pass her way (meaning Jesus would heal her). God honored the faith of that grandmother. The sweet lady wept and wept as her granddaughter walked back and forth across the platform, healed by the power of God. (Being a grandmother myself, I cannot resist adding: *Never underestimate the power of a praying grandmother!*)

God Uses Overshadowing to Heal (See Acts 5:15)

In New Testament days, during Peter's ministry, people would bring the sick and lay them alongside the path where he was to walk so that they would be healed when his shadow passed over or overshadowed them. This might sound like double talk if you don't understand the word "overshadow." It literally means to envelope in a haze of brilliancy or invest in preternatural influence.[4] A preternatural influence is one that is not explainable in the natural—it is supernatural.

This may be one of the least understood manifestations of God's healing power. I have seen this happen in large meetings where literally hundreds of people begin to fall under the power of God and healing takes place. This happened during a morning service in Brazil with 7,000 pastors in attendance. I felt the anointing to release this overshadowing anointing by simply saying, "Holy Spirit, come," and in one great wave about 500 pastors fell under the power of God.

God Heals Through the Anointing (See Isa. 10:27)

Sometimes the power of the Holy Spirit is so strong in a service that people are spontaneously healed without being prayed for—sometimes even without asking for a healing. Many Christian leaders, including myself, have actually seen the manifest presence of God. Of course, God is always present, but there are occasions when you can see His manifest presence through signs and wonders and through His glory as it falls upon people. This can include the overshadowing.

Ché Ahn, the leader of Harvest International Ministries in Pasadena, California, calls this the corporate power of God, which is the tangible power of the Holy Spirit manifested in the atmosphere of a given room or place.[5]

God is always present, but there are occasions when you actually can see His manifest presence through signs and wonders and through His glory as it falls upon people.

This kind of manifestation happens in Benny Hinn's meetings. Often people are healed because the atmosphere is charged with the power of God—it does not matter whether Benny is speaking in a large church building, a stadium or a tent erected on Hollywood Boulevard.

Years ago my husband, Mike, and I met with a famous healing evangelist from Argentina, Omar Cabrerra. His personal Holy Spirit adventures are legendary. For example, one time all of the patients in an entire clinic were healed when he prayed. He was best known for creative miracles where new toes or other body parts would grow on people. We asked Omar, "What brings about the manifest presence of God?" He answered, "Adoration of God." Omar went on to explain that God comes and inhabits His people when they allow themselves to be enveloped in His presence as they worship. When you praise God, He begins to heal.

When the anointing is manifest, many people will be healed without a word of knowledge, the laying on of hands or any other human act. Simply put, God's manifest glory alone releases healing.

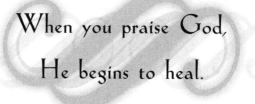

When you praise God,
He begins to heal.

God Gives Gifts of Healing (See 1 Cor. 23:9)
Every believer who is empowered by the Holy Spirit should pray for the sick. But some people have a special anointing from God. These people will operate in what the Bible identifies as the gift of healing. Peter Wagner offers this definition:

> The gift of healing is the special ability that God gives to certain members of the Body of Christ to serve as human intermediaries through whom it pleases God to cure illness and restore health apart from the use of natural means.[6]

If you have the gift of healing, it doesn't mean that you can heal anyone at anytime that you choose. If this was the way the gift worked, there would be people who regularly could go into hospitals and see everyone who is sick go home totally well. That does not happen. However, there are people like Omar Cabrerra who have a gift of healing, and at times they will see phenomenal numbers of people healed.

Certain ministry gifts will result in more people healed than others. For instance, in Acts 5:12 we learn that many signs and wonders occurred through the *hands* of the apostles. Also, there are healing evangelists whose primary gift is used by God to not only heal people but also to see them become born again.

Healing Happens Through the Working of Miracles (See Acts 5:12)
The working of miracles is a gift from God. When this gift is in operation, we see supernatural healing and manifestations of the power of God that are simply unexplainable in the natural realm.

Some time ago I was preaching at Harold and Cecilia Cabarellos's church in Guatemala City, Guatemala. It was quite an exciting time as people had come from all over the world to attend the congress.

When I entered the building, I noticed a wheelchair-bound elderly lady who was completely bundled up in blankets. As I passed her she didn't stir. I instantly petitioned God: "Lord, that is the one I want You to heal tonight. What a miracle that would be!"

During the meeting, the healing power of God swept through the large gathering and I asked for testimonies by those who had been healed. I turned and watched an elderly woman walk up the stairs and was astounded when I realized who she was! She was the elderly woman I had passed when I entered the meeting.

She walked up to me and testified that God had healed her legs, but the blindness in her eyes was only partially healed. I gazed into her beautiful blue eyes and noticed that they were glazed over with cataracts. I placed my hands over her eyes and simply said, "Be healed in the name of Jesus." What glorious words! A few moments later she looked around and a big grin formed on her face. She praised the Lord because He had healed her blindness. The woman must have been in her late 90s. What a precious reminder that God values and wants to heal everyone, whether young or old.

This was indeed a working of miracles.

Many times in my life I have been aware that the gift of miracles was in operation. It is hard to explain but when it is happening in healing meetings I do not doubt that the things that God says will come to pass. I know that the working of miracles couples with the gift of faith. These two gifts go hand in hand.

Soaking Prayers Produce Healing (See Luke 18:1-6)

There are certain movements that use what has been coined as "soaking prayers." The basic principle is that if you pray for a person once, and the power of God goes into him or her, then if you laid hands on that person a second or third time, a deeper dose of healing power will be sent. One of the people most known for this form of praying was John Wimber of the Vineyard movement.

While soaking prayer is not a biblical term, it is quite descriptive of how the power of God is released into a sick person. For example, soaking prayer teams will repeatedly visit a person who is terminally ill and lay hands on them. Sometimes the team members will pray in tongues over the person at the same time as they are laying on their hands.

Francis MacNutt is one of the advocates of this kind of praying and has seen marked improvement in people who have been prayed for in this way. MacNutt writes:

Praying for chronic ailments of long standing is, for example, usually a matter of continuing prayer over a long period of time.

Ordinarily, (again, not always) ailments such as arthritis are gradually healed. When parents ask for a mentally retarded child, I teach them how to pray every day, with the whole family, for the child. What usually seems to happen is that the child improves gradually—but much faster than the medical prognosis would call for. For long-term, deep-seated ailments a kind of "soaking prayer," repeated often, seems to bring the best results.[7]

I always encourage people to respond if there is a word of knowledge given concerning a certain sickness that they are fighting even if someone else has previously prayed for them. This is not a lack of faith. It may be that the person is operating with either the gift of healing or working of miracles by giving the word and they will receive their healing. I have known people who have prayed a number of times for healing and one day received a complete healing—as I noted, that happened with Evelyn Hamon. Prior to her actual healing, many people had prayed many times for her to be healed.

Healing Is Part of the Supernatural Life

Healing is part of living a supernatural life. We should expect to walk in the supernatural and pray for people to be healed and see miracles as well as to receive healing and miracles for ourselves. In the journaling section following this chapter, you can write about your experiences praying for the sick, the times that you have prayed for others and the times you have seen God heal a person.

Your Holy Spirit Adventures

Look over the types of prayer for healing listed in this chapter. Which types have you seen? Which ones have you done? Write down some outcomes and what you learned from God about healing in each experience.

How does God working in different ways to heal people strengthen your faith in Him. Why would we soak someone in prayer? How has this way of prayer effected you as you have prayed? Do you know someone who is sick? Can you pray for his or her healing right now?

THE GREAT
CLOUD OF
WITNESSES

As I have traveled and spoken at various places around the world, I have discovered some common threads that the Holy Spirit is weaving into the moves of God. One such thread is a great wave of the miraculous. Another is people studying past moves of God in specific geographic regions and then using the revelations of those movements as points of intercession for the present. Christians around the world are declaring, "God, do it again in our generation!"

In his powerful book *Digging the Wells of Revival*, Lou Engle wrote about this trend to bridge the past and the present. It is interesting to note how many healing revivals are being prophesied in various locations of the world where research has been done about the past great moves of God. For instance, Ken and Lois Gott have found that several great revivals had taken place in the Sunderland, England, area. One was with John Wesley and another was with Smith Wigglesworth. They also experienced what is called the Sunderland revival.

You Are Connected to Past Generations of Believers

There is also a strong connection to what can be called a great cloud of witnesses who have experienced mighty moves of God in the past. I have been concerned that many of today's young people and new believers who are being swept into the Kingdom might not know about some of the great revivalist and healing movements that have preceded the current move. The joining of the generations as well as a building upon the powerful foundational works of those who saw thousands and thousands of miracles is one of God's threads that is near and dear to my heart.

> Therefore we also, since we are surrounded by so great a cloud of witnesses, let us lay aside every weight, and the sin which so easily ensnares us, and let us run with endurance the race that is set before us (Heb. 12:1).

This verse refers to the great hall of faith noted in Hebrews 11. The picture is of godly patriarchs like Moses and Abraham and women like Sarah who lived in earlier times. These great leaders now watch as spectators and witnesses of the race run by the current generation. The "cloud" is a well-known and accepted analogy of the ancient times during which these onlookers lived. The weights refer to those things that hinder the actual running of the race.

Witnesses from generations past are at this moment peering down from heaven's balcony and cheering the race today's generations run.

Witnesses from generations past are at this moment peering down from heaven's balcony and cheering the race today's generations run. I believe there are times when God draws back the veil that separates the earthly and heavenly realms so that that cloud of witnesses can rejoice.

There is a race that believers run today. I hear the heart cry of my fellow Christians who want to see the greater works the Lord said believers would do after He went to be with the Father (see John 14:12). What are these works? They certainly include the dead rising, the blind seeing, the lame walking and countless other glorious proofs that Jesus is the living God!

As I have studied Hebrews 12:1, it has occurred to me that one of the weights that believers need to put aside to run the race is that of ignorance of this cloud of witnesses. This cloud is occupied not only by biblical patriarchs, but also by saints of all generations. Just as the Hebrews 11 hall of faith is inspiring, there are some people who lived in past generations who certainly could be included to lift us to a higher place of belief that God is the same yesterday, today and forever! (see Heb. 13:8). The ranks of saints in the cloud of witness might include people like John G. Lake, Smith Wigglesworth, Maria Woodworth-Etter and many others.

When I was first learning that God heals today, I poured over the Scriptures that explain the miraculous. At one point I went to the local Christian bookstore in search of more information. A precious woman named Joyce Bogle managed the store. God used her to steer me to books about the miraculous. As I studied biographies of the great healing evangelists and their writings, next to paragraphs about the mighty works God did through them I wrote comments like "Lord, I want to do these things, too!"

John Lake Set the Pace

One day I came home with the book *Dominion over Demons, Disease, and Death* by Gordon Lindsay. As I perused the book, I read a story about John Lake's faith that simply stunned me. The story is also told in other books about his life. Lake was a missionary to South Africa in the early 1900s. In January 1920, a terrible plague swept the nation. In less than a month, one quarter of the population had died. In fact, the plague was so contagious that the government offered $1,000 to any nurse who would care for the sick. Lake and one assistant went to help, free of charge. He and one assistant went into houses, brought out the dead and buried them. But no symptom of the plague ever touched them.[1]

God Uses Lake in Africa

This amazing phenomenon came to the attention of a doctor who wanted to know the secret of Lake's protection from the plague. Lake, of course, informed him that it was none other than the power of Jesus Christ. He then proposed a bold experiment. The doctor was to take the bloody froth from a dead plague victim and put it under a microscope to make certain that it was virulent. Then Lake put this same bloody foam on his hand. He explained, "You can fill [the palm of] my hand with them and I will keep it under the microscope and instead of these germs remaining alive, they will die instantly."[2] It happened just as he said it would.

Lake believed the promise found in Luke 10:19:

Behold, I give you authority to trample on serpents and scorpions, and over all the power of the enemy, and nothing shall by any means hurt you.

The power of God that healed so many through this man of God killed the germs as it surged through his hand. Who was this unusual man? John Graham Lake was born on March 18, 1870, in Ontario, Canada. At 16, he was born again in a Salvation Army meeting in Michigan. His life was full of tragedy. As a youth, 8 of his 16 siblings became ill and died.

We grow excited to see the emphasis God is placing on the marketplace today, but in his day Lake was also a successful business consultant. In the coming move of God we will see what I call a marriage or partnership where healing moves into the marketplace and we see many in the business world doing signs and wonders.

Lake Moves into the Healing Ministry

Lake became involved with John Alexander Dowie's healing rooms in Chicago and was healed of rheumatism. As a result of what he learned there, others in his family, including his wife, Jennie, were also healed.

After a tremendous experience with the Holy Spirit, Lake went to Africa where he had a great healing ministry. He later returned to the United States and settled in Spokane, Washington. It was in Spokane that he established healing rooms where, over a five-year period, about 100,000 healings occurred. According to Cal Pierce of the Healing Rooms ministry, the city of Spokane was declared to be the healthiest city in America sometime between 1915 and 1920, during Lake's ministry there. It is attributed to the many healings that took place. In fact, this standing continues to this day as *Men's Health Magazine* ranked Spokane the 16th healthiest city for males.[3]

The Healing Rooms Are Reopened

My friends Cal and Michelle Pierce were called of God to reopen these healing rooms at the same location in Spokane and expand the movement around the world. As of this writing there are 200 associated healing rooms in 15 nations, including India, Great Britain and Israel.

If you go to one of the healing rooms, you will be received in a room that looks very much like a doctor's office. Then you will be asked to fill out a form that describes your symptoms. Healing practitioners will use this information. Next, you will be ushered into a room in which three people will pray for your healing. These practitioners have been taught to go for the root or problem that allowed the particular sickness to enter your body. This is very similar to what John Lake did when he and his wife ministered healing.

Cal and Michelle Pierce have found that there are root causes that allow certain kinds of sicknesses to enter a person's body and they have written a manual for their workers. Once they deal with the root, they begin to pray for healing.

In another room, intercessors continually pray for the power of God to be present in the healing rooms. When I visited the rooms, I was deeply touched by the fact that no charge is ever made for the prayer and it is first come, first served. There is no preference given to certain people. Many miracles have taken place as the Pierces and their practitioners have redug John G. Lake's well of revival. In my opinion, healing should be accessible to everyone at anytime. People don't get sick at convenient times. Yet churches often only offer healing prayers during Sunday services—sometimes not even then. It would be wonderful if churches in cities all over the world would one day have places set aside to pray for the sick on a 24-hour basis alongside their 24-hour prayer rooms.

24-Hour Prayer Should Be Offered

One day the Lord spoke to me about this when I was ministering in England. He said that He wants a 24-hour church because He is a 24-hour God. He went on to say, "My people lock their buildings and do not have a place for those in need to be ministered to." The lost do not want to get saved during convenient office hours. I believe that in the coming move of God healing, salvation, comforting the brokenhearted, intercessory prayer and worship will take place 24 hours a day, seven days a week.

I realize there needs to be a release of thousands of dollars to fund this kind of vision. I also pray that there will be people who retire early from secular jobs so that they can give their lives to such activities. People are retiring earlier and living longer; this means that many people still have many productive years left after they leave the workforce.

John Alexander Dowie Helped Change Cities for God

As I already noted, John Alexander Dowie affected Lake. I want to take a look at Dowie because of some things that I see happening in the next supernatural move of God that will affect whole cities.

Dowie was born on May 25, 1847, in Edinburgh, Scotland. He was sick most of his childhood until he studied about healing. His ministry took him to Australia for a season and finally to America. He was not only a healing evangelist but also a church reformer—he left the Congregational church to start his own denomination called the Christian Catholic Church. Because Dowie was a reformer, much can be learned from him as the Church around the world moves into another time of great transformation and reformation.

Dowie Moves to Chicago

Dowie set up the headquarters of his church in Chicago. When the 1893 World's Fair opened in Chicago, he built a little hut outside the gates and began to pray for the sick. So many people were getting healed that crowds gathered. People wanted to witness the miracles. A local newspaper started a campaign against Dowie. As part of the campaign, it published lists of ministers and others who were opposed to Dowie's healing hut. None of this moved Dowie. In fact, he expanded his outreach.

So many people came to Chicago for the World's Fair that there were not enough places for them to stay. In response, Dowie started rooming houses that he called "healing homes."

In 1895, Dowie was arrested for "practicing medicine without a license." He was repeatedly arrested (some say 100 times). Nonetheless, he did not stop praying for the sick. And he did not limit his ministry to praying for the sick.

Dowie felt that God had called him to build a city. That call became reality on January 1, 1900, when he started the Zion Land Investment Association. Everyone who wanted to lease land in his city (they could not purchase land there) had to follow strict rules. No one could drink liquor, use tobacco or eat pork.

God Is Calling City Builders

I do believe that God is going to call some Christians in the last days to be city builders and societal reformers. Bishop Bill Hamon prophesied this in 1975 in his book *The Eternal Church*.

Many leaders in the healing movements have caught the attention of whole cities as Dowie did in Chicago. He could have had a major influence on that society for good; instead he fell into grave error—he actually thought that he was Elijah returned. Nonetheless, there is still much to be learned from his tenacity and reformation anointing. In addition, Dowie's story demonstrates the need to stay in relationships with other strong Christians who will speak into your life and offer correction.

In this coming move of God many people will leverage the favor that comes with God's healing and step forward to impact their society. In studying the great healing revivalists, I have noted that oftentimes

> In this coming move of God many people will leverage the favor that comes with God's healing and step forward to impact their society.

mayors and other government officials would be touched by the move of God. This opens up great opportunities to talk about the transformation of cities.

Maria Woodworth-Etter Reached the Masses

One contemporary of Dowie's who remained faithful to the call was Maria Woodworth-Etter. Etter was born in New Lisbon, Ohio, on July 22, 1844. She was one of the women whose life inspired Pentecostal pioneer Aimee Semple McPherson. The two women met in Indianapolis where Etter was preaching.

Etter also had an impact on me. She serves as an example of someone who demonstrated God's power to the masses. I am blessed to report that many of the ways she saw God move have also happened as I have traveled to the nations.

To those of you who have a call of God on your life, don't be afraid to ask God for great things. When my children were napping, I would often kneel down beside my bed and pray. I would ask God to use me to help bring revival in the nations. God took those prayers and began to move to open doors for me to speak and see many mighty miracles.

One day when I was preaching to a thousand pastors in Mar del Plata, Argentina, the Holy Spirit spoke gently to my heart: "This is what you prayed for. You opened this door on your knees in prayer."

Maria Woodworth-Etter's book *Signs and Wonders* was a jumping off place for my intercession. I would read her book and then write my name in the margin, "Lord, I want to do those things that she did. I want to see souls saved, lives changed and powerful miracles performed." I would pray the Scripture in Mark 11:24:

> Therefore I say to you, whatever things you ask when you pray, believe that you receive them, and you will have them.

Years later, as I reread Etter's book in preparation for writing my own book, I realized that standing on that promise brought great results. One of the things that most touched my life about her ministry was the way she listened to the Holy Spirit. At the beginning of the ministry as she prepared for the call, she thought that God would simply open doors for her to preach. However, as she prayed it became clear that God wanted her to do something to reach out to the harvest field before any door was open. How could she do such a thing?

God Says "Go"

As she prayed, the Lord told her to go and that He would be with her. "Where?" she inquired of the Lord. Jesus again said, "Go, and I will be with you. Go here, go there, wherever souls are perishing."[4]

And that is precisely what she did.

Many young ministers think that they have to wait to be invited somewhere to preach. Not so! There are many white harvest fields in cities around the world. Find a place with no church or a people who have never heard and begin preaching there. Hold a job in the day and preach at night. Visit your neighbors and love them into the kingdom! You do not have to be a preacher to follow this principle. Anyone can go anywhere God calls on them to go.

Etter was pro-active and obedient. She wrote about one scenario:

On Sunday I would ride seven miles [I assume by horseback] and hold meetings on Saturday evening, and three meetings on Sabbath—sometimes in different churches—and then ride home over a hilly and rough road. By this time I would be nearly exhausted and hardly able to walk around to do my work. But the last of the week I would go again; and often through the week I held meetings in the towns around where I was born and raised, where we had lived since we were married.[5]

Oh, the glamour of the ministry! Much of what God asks you to do is simply hard work, but it produces great results.

Etter was known for demonstrations of the power of God in unusual ways. As she was preaching, people would run to the altar screaming for mercy. Men and women would fall under the power of God and lay on the floor as though dead. One time, while preaching in a house, people were laying around as dead. After about two hours, one person after another suddenly sprang to his or her feet and shouted. In every room, people stood and worshiped God and their faces were shiny. Etter called these bright conversions. In those days of revival she said that all the churches would come out in a given city and "we could not tell a Baptist from a Brethren."[6]

> There are many white harvest fields in cities around the world. Find a place with no church or a people who have never heard and begin preaching there.

God Shakes a City

One lovely and dramatic incident occurred January 1, 1885, in a Methodist church. The church had been rather cold and formal (according to Etter) when five of the leading members united in prayer that God would shake the city as well as the surrounding countryside. God answered in an amazing way through a little boy from the church. This is how Etter told the story:

> The class-leader's little boy fell under the power of God first. He rose up, stepped on the pulpit, and began to talk with the wisdom and power of God. His father began to shout and praise the Lord. As the little fellow exhorted and asked the people to come to Christ they began to weep all over the house. Some shouted; others fell prostrated.[7]

This display of power touched places of business—including saloons—and reached sinners from all walks of life. Indeed, the whole countryside was affected. Many people fell down under the power of God—not only in church but on highways, in their homes and in businesses. These unusual meetings went on for five weeks.

Isaiah 11:6 is poetic, but it also reveals a power truth: "A little child shall lead them." I know that in the coming days, there will be revivals sparked by the testimonies and preaching of little children just like that boy did in 1885.

There are many great stories from Maria Woodworth-Etter's time. God also used her powerfully in signs and wonders, specifically via physical healings. Her ministry had a great impact on many people, including F. F. Bosworth, who wrote *Christ the Healer*. It has also been reported that Smith Wigglesworth was influenced by Etter and even picked up some of her favorite sayings.

Smith Wigglesworth Increases Everyone's Faith

Wigglesworth presents to us one of the most outstanding examples of faith toward God and belief in His power to heal. In fact, Wigglesworth has been called the Twentieth Century Apostle of Faith. In the late 1970s, I read his book *Ever Increasing Faith* and was deeply inspired by it.

My husband, Mike, and I have been to Sunderland, England, where we met Lois Gott. Lois's father had served in ministry under Wigglesworth. It has been said that Wigglesworth raised 13 people from the dead, but some people believe that the total was actually much higher.

Wigglesworth was uneducated and a plumber by trade. Lois has letters from him that contain many misspelled words—he spelled "holy" h-o-l-l-y. He admitted that he could not spell. However, he didn't need to be able to spell to be used of God to manifest His glory.

He was born in 1859 in a humble shack in Menston, Yorkshire, England. At eight years of age he was converted in a Wesleyan Methodist meeting which he attended with his devout grandmother. He, in turn, was instrumental in his own mother's conversion. When he was 13, his parents moved to Bradford where he began working with the Salvation Army. When he was twenty, Wigglesworth moved to Liverpool where he ministered to scores of poor children in dock sheds. Hundreds of them were saved. In the early years of ministry, it was Polly Wigglesworth who was the preacher and Smith the personal worker in the little mission they operated in Bradford.[8]

As I read this story about Wigglesworth, I thought of how, like Maria Woodworth-Etter, he did not wait for ministry to come to him, but rather found a need and filled it. The children in the dock sheds needed Christ and Wigglesworth became the answer. In every city there is a need somewhere that you could be the answer to, whether it is leading a Bible study, or counseling, or visiting hospitals.

I Follow Wigglesworth's Lead

I started my own worldwide ministry by teaching children's church and leading worship in our little church in Weatherford, Texas. Each Sunday I would get there early to rehearse the worship team before service, lead the worship from the piano and then slip away to teach the children by myself. At the last minute I would slip back into the main sanctuary and help end the service. I thrived on this ministry regimen! Children were praying for people who had one leg shorter than the other and the short legs were growing! One child's body was completely covered with mosquito bites and she was completely healed. About 100 children or so born again in one year and the church only had 200 members, including the children.

Here is my point: Many people are waiting for someone to open a door for them when there are unlocked doors everywhere waiting for someone to open them. One day the Lord gave me a prophecy that said, "You are not waiting on me—I am waiting on you!"

Wigglesworth heard that people were receiving the power of the Holy Spirit and speaking in tongues in Sunderland under the ministry of Vicar Alexander Boddy. He went to Sunderland to check it out. At first he was disappointed by what he found as it seemed there wasn't much of God's fire. Wanting a Pentecostal experience, he disrupted the meeting so many times that he was disciplined.

Discouraged and ready to leave Sunderland, Wigglesworth went to talk with the Vicar's wife and to say good-bye. He was disappointed that he had not received the gift of tongues. She answered, "It is not tongues you need, but the baptism."[9] She proceeded to pray for him and the fire fell from heaven on him. He had a vision of the Cross and began to worship and speak in tongues.

Wigglesworth went home so changed that when he stood in the pulpit his wife was astounded by the change in him, as she had previously felt that she was as much filled with the Holy Spirit as her husband had been.

The People Laughed in Church

At the end of the service, the people were laughing. This was not ordinary laughter like what happens after a joke is told; rather, this was a holy laughter given in response to the power of the Holy Spirit. It was joyful laughter and it filled the place. After a while 11 people were on the floor laughing in the Spirit. Some people feel that holy laughter is a modern-day phenomenon of the Spirit, but it is not at all new! This was part of the demonstration of the power of the Holy Spirit in that day as well.

I had believed that God would do through me the same things that He had done through the great evangelists.

Wigglesworth's key to the mighty miracles he saw can be found in two words: *only believe!* He explained it this way, "There is something about believing God that makes God willing to pass over a million people just to anoint you."[10]

The Saints Movement Is Underway

When I read that quote I realized that in my younger days I had tapped into this way of faith. I had believed that God would do through me the same things that He had done through the great evangelists. Only a few of these things have actually happened, but I expect them all and more to manifest during my lifetime.

We are moving into what I have heard Bishop Bill Hamon call "the saints movement." This is where every believer will demonstrate the power of God in our society. There was a time when the kind of things that I write about in this book only happened in large revival meetings, but the move of God is changing. I know that one day Christian youth will pray in their schools and mighty signs and wonders will take place. I dream of the day when there will be healing rooms right in our schools. It will only take a few notable miracles for school administrators to change their minds concerning prayer and Bible reading in the classroom.

Another principle of faith that Wigglesworth implemented was acting on the Word of God. He would preach on a certain passage and then tell people to act on what they had heard.

> For example, at a meeting in Arizona, a young woman was healed of tuberculosis. When she stepped into the aisle, Wigglesworth said, "Now I am going to pray for you and then you run around this building." He prayed, then he shouted, "Run woman. Run!" The woman said, "But I cannot run. I can scarcely stand." "Don't talk back to me," Wigglesworth shouted, "Do as I have said." She was reluctant, so Wigglesworth jumped down from the platform, grabbed her, and began running. She clung to him until she gathered speed, then galloped around the auditorium without any effort.[11]

While this may seem radical, it was really the gift of faith in operation. Wigglesworth knew that if she ran, she'd be healed.

This book is about living supernatural lives for God. Wigglesworth put it like this:

> You can never be ordinary from the day you receive the life from above. You become extraordinary from the day you receive this life from above. You become extraordinary, filled with the extraordinary power of our extraordinary God.[12]

Aimee Semple McPherson Was a Forerunner and an Innovator

I am going to include Aimee Semple McPherson in this chapter because, unlike others, she not only had a traveling ministry, but she also founded a local church and a denomination. She was an amazing innovator and an apostle. Aimee was born on October 9, 1890, near Salford, Ontario, Canada. Her mother married her father when he was 50 and her mother was 15. The day after the marriage, Aimee's mother got on her knees and prayed this prayer:

> If you will only hear my prayer, as you heard Hannah's prayer of old, and give me a little baby girl, I will give her unreservedly into your service, that she may preach the Word I should have preached, . . . O Lord, hear and answer me.[13]

God answered her with a little girl who would grow up to change the world.

I believe many mothers are praying similar prayers today. I know that my parents lost a child before I was born, and that they prayed together and asked God to give them a little girl. Today, I am preaching as my daddy did and he is one of those who now make up the great cloud of witnesses in heaven.

Aimee married a handsome young man named Robert and they went to Macao, which, though owned by China now, was a Portuguese settlement then. Tragedy struck and they both arrived ill. Robert died and not long afterward, Aimee delivered her own little baby, Roberta Star.

Aimee Hears from God

God had to deal with Aimee in a strong way after she came home from China with Roberta and married Harold McPherson. Although she had accepted the call to preach, she listened to those who said she could not do so and needed to be a stay-at-home mother. Finally, after she had a second child, Rolf, her health broke and she became ill. After undergoing a serious operation, Aimee's health deteriorated to such a degree that the doctors assigned her to the room where they put the dying. As her life was slipping away she heard from God: "Now will you go?" Here is the story in Aimee's own words:

> In the early hours of the morning, I realized that I was either going into the grave or out into the field with the gospel. I made my decision and gasped out the words, "Yes—Lord—I'll go!"[14]

After she made this promise to the Lord she was completely healed.

I want to insert here that this story had a great impact on me when I was a young mother. Even though I knew that God had called me to preach, I could not bring myself to commit to the ministry because my children were so small. Madison (also known as Mary) and Daniel were

2 and 5 when I started to preach. The Lord kept prodding me with Matthew 10:37-39:

He who loves father or mother more than Me is not worthy of Me. And he who loves son or daughter more than Me is not worthy of Me. And he who does not take his cross and follow after Me is not worthy of Me. He who finds his life will lose it, and he who loses his life for My sake will find it.

Aimee's story not only gave me courage to say yes to the call, but it also put the fear of the Lord upon my life to not resist. Aimee Semple McPherson accomplished so much in her short life. Sadly, she died young, at the age of 53.

God's Healing Comes to Los Angeles

So many people were healed through her ministry that I went to visit Angelus Temple to pray several years ago. I saw evidence of the medical apparatus left after the miracles at Angelus Temple in Los Angeles. While that aspect of her ministry is more well known, here are a few other amazing facts:

Aimee founded one of the first Christian radio stations in the world, KFSG, which ran Christian programming from its founding in 1923 until it went off the air in 2003. The church she built (Angelus Temple) was not a simple sanctuary but a theater for God and today serves as the International Church of the Foursquare Gospel headquarters.

When other denominations refused to ordain women, she founded the Church of the Foursquare Gospel and 1,000 pastors joined the first day!

Angelus Temple seated 5,000 people when it was finished in late 1922. It included a prayer tower where people could pray around the clock. The church also had a 100-voice choir and a brass band. Aimee captured the attention of everyone from ordinary people to Hollywood stars such as Mary Pickford, Anthony Quinn and Charlie Chaplin.

As I read Aimee's story, one thing that most impressed me was the children's church of a 1,000 where the children did the preaching and leading of music. Aimee's son, Rolf, was a child at that time and he would participate in the service, too!

> Innovation was Aimee's middle name! Is it any wonder that I call her an apostle?

Innovation was Aimee's middle name! Is it any wonder that I call her an apostle? Reading about her accomplishments was like seeing an account of the vision of God that He is speaking to the Church today. We are called to affect Hollywood and the entire media, touch the children with a great revival, establish 24-hour prayer, and release the miraculous.

God Uses Ordinary People to Accomplish Extraordinary Deeds

I could include many healing evangelists in this chapter. Others like Kathryn Kuhlman, William Branham, and in more recent times, Oral Roberts, all led extraordinary ministries. If you are hungry to see the power of God move in your life you would benefit from reading about these great men and women of God.

Indeed, we are called to live extraordinary lives. Reading about these great leaders not only gives us great faith, but it also gives us impartation. I pray that you will not be content with a mediocre, mundane life; rather, you will be full of the Holy Spirit and do supernatural exploits for God.

Your Holy Spirit Adventures

Which one of the great men and women whose stories are told in this chapter has inspired you the most? Why? How will their supernatural lives' inspire you to live a supernatural life?

Dowie was a city builder for God. What would happen in your city if large numbers of people were healed? What if miracles happened in the marketplace? Has God given you a vision for your city? Even if it is vague, start now by writing some notes about what God is speaking to your heart about your city.

OF COURSE,
I WILL, PRAY FOR
YOUR HORSE,

A few years ago I lived in a small town in Texas named Weatherford. Horses were and are very important to quite a few people in that area. One day I went to visit the home of a married couple I knew from church. The wife was born again and we had been praying for God to touch her husband's heart in a way that would cause him to consider Jesus as his Savior.

When I entered their farmhouse, one of the children ran up to me and cried out, "Miss Cindy! Miss Cindy!" (That is the polite way for little Texan children to address a grown-up that they love, but use of the first name without the "Miss" part doesn't show proper respect.)

"Miss Cindy, our horse is sick and can't get up!" the child exclaimed. I knew enough about horses to realize that this was not a good sign. Then it struck me! This could be the very thing that God was going to use to touch their daddy's heart. I could actually see myself going out to that pasture and laying hands on their horse, and I could see the horse getting up and running around.

Some of you know me, others don't; so I will add some explanation as I describe what I did. That day, I was wearing dress shoes and nice clothes. As you can imagine, it was and is unusual for me to crawl under or over a ranch fence in that attire. However, praying for the animal could affect a person's soul, so as far as I was concerned, who cared if I ruined my nearly new shoes. This was a matter of eternity!

"Show me your horse!" I gallantly said. The little children started jumping up and down because they knew Miss Cindy must believe that God was going to heal their pet horse!

I must admit that as I walked through that Texas pasture, careful not to tread upon any cow patties (if you are from another place where you don't know what they are, I need only explain that they are made from that which comes from the back end of a cow), I started to have some trepidation. By this time in my Christian walk I had laid hands on a number of humans but never on a horse.

Finally, after crawling under a wire fence and over the corral fence, the children, the mother and I arrived at the downed horse. By this time I was getting excited. This could be the very thing that would turn the heart of their daddy and I felt full of faith!

Bending over, I put both of my hands on the horse's side (I avoided the front end because he had teeth and we weren't acquainted with each other), and boldly said, "Be healed in the name of Jesus!" We waited breathlessly.

All of a sudden the horse got his hind legs up, pushed and stood! He was healed from that day on. The most glorious part was that it did touch their daddy's heart, and he became not only born again but a fine leader in the church.

Prophetic evangelism is one of the most powerful means we have in the Body of Christ to help reap the harvest.

The point is that God knows what circumstance will cause the heart of a person to turn to Him. Likewise, people know that secret place that causes them to understand that God intimately cares for them. I call this prophetic evangelism.

God Is Preparing a Great Harvest

Prophetic evangelism is hearing God's voice and understanding His instruction, then being used as His instrument to communicate in such a way that lost individuals connect with the God who loves them.

Many Christians have prayed for years for a great revival of souls across the nations. Prophetic evangelism is one of the most powerful means we have in the Body of Christ to help reap the harvest. You might say that it is a sickle, or tool, in the hand of God to reap the whitened fields.

As I have traveled around the world, I have noticed how the themes of harvest and transformation have become a rallying cry. A key passage for this cry is Matthew 9:37-38:

> The harvest truly is plentiful, but the laborers are few. Therefore pray the Lord of the harvest to send out laborers into His harvest.

Intercession ripens the harvest. During the late 1980s and the 1990s, large numbers of prayer movements arose in which believers cried out for revival. I was in many of these meetings—perhaps you were, too.

God Prioritizes the Harvest

While studying Matthew 9:37-38, I came to understand a key point in intercession for harvest. Just as we might invoke Jehovah Rapha or Jehovah Jirah for healing, the powerful name to be used to see thousands saved is Lord of the Harvest.

In the introduction of this book I noted that one reason I have been led of the Lord to write on the subject of the supernatural was that we are close to another Jesus People Movement. You might even be reading this book while this has already happened and you are in the middle of such a move of God.

Nations that have very few Christians will see explosive growth in numbers of born-again believers. This new wave of the Holy Spirit will hit nation after nation and prophetic evangelism and learning how to flow with God through the supernatural will be used mightily.

Even Unwed Pregnant Women Need Christ

My friend Ché Ahn related a story to me about how God used him in prophetic evangelism:

Years ago, I was part of an outreach to the University of Maryland. We were giving out free snacks, drinks such as apple cider and such. During that time I looked up and noticed a young woman coming out of the Student Union building. At that moment God gave me a supernatural word of knowledge [this is information that the giver has no natural knowledge about]. God spoke in a flash of thought: *That girl is pregnant, considering an abortion, and she has already had one before this.*

What would you do if God gave you that kind of information about another person? You see, sometimes God tells you insider info for you to simply pray over, but in the case of prophetic evangelism He gives it to you to do something with it. Ché prayed (I'm sure he fervently prayed), "God, how am I going to tell her?"

Ché then started to walk toward her. How would you feel at that moment? Walking in the supernatural involves taking risks and it requires spiritual diplomacy. As Ché approached the young woman he said, "Hello, I'm a pastor. Please don't be offended, but I sense God told me that you are with child. God loves you, and you are considering an abortion. In fact, this is your second time."

At that the young woman broke down weeping, and through her sobs she said, "How did you know? My boyfriend doesn't even know!" The power of the kingdom of God had just manifested itself in that young woman's life.

From that point on Ché had a receptive audience to be able to share about salvation and the love of Christ. The young woman became a campus ministry leader. Moreover, her boyfriend also became born again and a ministry leader. There is absolutely no telling how many people will be in heaven as a result of that one word of knowledge.

Why Did Zacchaeus Come Down from the Tree?
Jesus himself gave us the example of the power of prophetic evangelism:

> Then Jesus entered and passed through Jericho. Now behold, there was a man named Zacchaeus who was a chief tax collector, and he was rich. And he sought to see who Jesus was, but could not because of the crowd, for he was of short stature. So he ran ahead and climbed up into a sycamore tree to see Him, for He was going to pass that way. And when Jesus came to the place, He looked up and saw him, and said to him, "Zacchaeus, make haste and come down, for today I must stay at your house" (Luke 19:1-10).

What astounding revelation! First, Jesus knew the man's name. He picked him out of the crowd by name. Second, Zacchaeus was considered the lowest of the low to the Jewish people as he had gotten rich by extortion. Not only was he a tax collector, but he was a *chief* tax collector—not worthy of anything but the disdain of all the people.

Perhaps you have read the parable found in Luke 18:9-14. The two people in the illustration are a Pharisee and a tax collector. The Pharisee stood and prayed, "God, I thank You that I am not like other men—extortioners, unjust, adulterers, or even as this tax collector. I fast twice a week; I give tithes of all that I possess."

And the tax collector, standing far off, would not so much as raise his eyes to heaven, but beat his breast saying, "God, be merciful to me a sinner!'

This parable illustrates the love of Christ using prophetic evangelism by means of a word of knowledge. During those few seconds the power of the love of God reached out and said to Zacchaeus, "You have worth to me. Even though you are hated by all men, you are a sell-out, and you are considered the scum of the earth; the Son of God sees you and knows you!"

No wonder that Zacchaeus came down out of the tree as fast as he could. He had great joy! He was loved by God!

The crowd evidentially didn't like Jesus' behavior because the gossip group started and they murmured, "He has gone to be a guest with a man who is a sinner." As I read the story of Zacchaeus while writing this book it came alive to me again. I had sung Sunday School songs about him as a tiny girl in church, but I never saw the story like I did this time. Jesus hadn't told him he had to become a follower, nor had He rebuked him for sinfulness. He simply reached deep into the wilderness and loneliness in the heart of a despised tax collector and knew his name!

That is all it took for a life-changing transaction to take place in Zacchaeus's life. Zacchaeus stood in the midst of the crowd and said to the Lord, "Look, Lord, I give half of my goods to the poor; and if I have taken anything from anyone by false accusation, I restore fourfold." Conviction came upon him through love rather than through condemnation.

God Works in Unexpected Ways

If you had walked in to the restaurant, at first glance the people there would have appeared to be rather normal. You might have recognized the actress standing in line for the women's restroom, but you probably would not have realized that she was actually a supernatural being. The actress—my friend Jamie Lyn Bauer—eats at fast-food restaurants, drives Southern California's freeways and shops at malls. She looks and acts quite natural, but she actually lives a supernatural life, as do many others like her.

That day, while waiting in the women's restroom line, Jamie met a young woman. She listened to the young woman's story about her struggles in her marriage and her questions about God. Jamie eventually spent 45 minutes talking, praying and releasing the power of God into the woman's life.

This is where the supernatural realm took over. Jamie's prayer sounded something like this: "Father, You are our healer, our Savior, our deliverer. In the name of Jesus Christ, I take authority over the spirit that would divide this couple. Divorce, you have no place here. You must leave this woman right now. I speak life and wholeness into this woman right now!"

As Jamie prayed, she had specific words of knowledge from God for the woman. How can this happen? What makes people like Jamie so different? How can they pray in this way? *They have the power of the supernatural operating in their lives and they know how to release it.*

After releasing God's power into the woman's life, Jamie went on her way, not knowing exactly what God would do. Some time later, the woman wrote to Jamie and described how she had recommitted her life to Christ and how her marriage had been healed. A prayer said on behalf of a stranger is not as dramatic as some other Holy Spirit adventure stories, but I include it here to show how God can use any Christian to

Jamie looks and acts quite natural, but she actually lives a supernatural life.

release His supernatural power in lives everywhere every day. Moreover, when you live a supernatural life—as Jamie does—God will surprise you by using you in unexpected ways and in unlikely places—even in line waiting for the women's restroom.

When Wigglesworth Prophesied People Were Evangelized

The famous healing evangelist, Smith Wigglesworth tells a great story in his book *Ever Increasing Faith*. It happened when he went to Australia to minister. In those days (after the turn of the twentieth century) people had to take long ocean voyages when they went from continent to continent. He tells this story of hearing the voice of God and the resulting conversion of a man on his ship:

> When you are filled with the Spirit, you will know the voice of God.

[He goes on to explain people would swarm the boat to sell goods at Alden and Bombay. Among the goods were beautiful carpets and all kinds of oriental goods.]

At one point there was a man selling some ostrich feathers. As I was looking over the side of the ship watching the trading, a gentleman said to me, "Would you go shares with me in buying that bunch of feathers?" What did I want with feathers? I had no use for such things and no room for them either. But the gentleman put the question to me again, "Will you go shares with me in buying that bunch?" The Spirit of God said to me, "Do it."

The price of the feathers was three pounds, but the gentleman said, "I have no money with me, but if you will pay the man for them, I will send the cash down to you by the purser." I paid for the feathers and gave the gentleman his share. I said to him, "No, please don't give that money to the purser; I want you to bring it to me personally to my cabin." I said to the Lord, "What about these feathers?" He showed me that he had a purpose in my purchasing them.

At about ten o'clock the gentleman came to my cabin and said, "I've brought the money." I said to him, "It is not your money that I want; it is your soul that I am seeking for God." Right there he opened up the whole plan of his life and began to seek God; and that morning he wept his way through to God.[1]

I have also been told Smith Wigglesworth had a unique, prophetic way to evangelize at a crossroads. As the story goes, Wigglesworth would stand at the crossing and watch for souls. As each cart would pass by he would say to the Lord, "Are they ready, is this the one?" He knew that the Holy Spirit knew who was ready to be born again and who was not. Wigglesworth was fishing for souls. He partnered with God in this and God knows how to catch fish. When the Spirit would say to him something to the effect of "They are ready," he would jump into the cart with the person and lead them to the Lord.

I have taken this as my model for prophetic evangelism. Each day as I go about my daily walk, I ask the Lord this question, "Where is my harvest?" By this I mean those people who are ready to meet the Lord and those he wants me to witness to.

God Stretched My Idea of Evangelism

Some time ago I became deeply convicted that I only led people to the Lord from the platform while preaching. While I was on the plane or in public places I didn't want to be bothered. I think that I had become full of my own self-importance and visibility. What was wrong? I was no longer following the example of Christ who told us to leave the 99 and go after the one lost sheep (see Matt. 18:11-14). It is probably a familiar passage to you, but it is so beautiful that I am going to copy it here for you:

> For the Son of Man has come to seek and save that which was lost. What do you think? If a man has a hundred sheep, and one of them goes astray, does he not leave the ninety-nine and go to the mountains to seek the one that is straying? And if he should find it, assuredly, I say to you, he rejoices more over that sheep than over the ninety-nine that did not go astray. Even so it is not

the will of your Father who is in heaven that one of these little ones should perish.

The truth is that we, as Christians, usually live a very insulated life. We don't want to be around those sinners who swear, do bad things and act like sinners. In many cases we have developed a subculture where we hardly touch those who are lost. Rather, we move in and out of society with non-Christians serving us in restaurants, at gas stations and in the store where we buy our groceries without really seeing them as people who need Christ. I was guilty of all those things, always in a hurry, always busy.

It wasn't that I didn't regularly see people accept Christ. I did—by the hundreds and hundreds. Yet, on a personal level I had a hardened heart. If someone had asked me if I cared, I would have said, "Of course, look how many I've led to Christ in the last few weeks."

Good Intentions Are Not Enough

The truth is, as I had done, many Christians have abdicated from the world on a personal level. Donald Posterski explains it well: "Often out of good intentions to be godly, they have confused the biblical injunction to be separate with social segregation. They let the activities of church and relationships with fellow Christians dominate their lives. They sense that the world is dangerous to their faith instead of cultivating meaningful contact with the very people who would benefit from life with serious Christians."[2] The Holy Spirit is still crying out through John 17:18:

As You sent Me into the world, I also have sent them into the world.

I like what my friend Ed Silvoso, author of *That None Should Perish*, preaches, "We expect some great wind to come and blow the harvest right in the door of the church, when, in truth, they are not going to come to us, we need to go to them."[3]

As I meditated on this truth, I realized that the Bible teaches that the *fields* are white with harvest, not the *church building*. You have to go out into the fields that you have prayed so fervently to see harvested!

> You have to go out into the fields that you have prayed so fervently to see harvested!

After I became deeply convicted of the fact that I mainly saw the harvest field in the auditoriums and stadiums where I was preaching, I became aware of the people around me. I saw them in a much different light. I saw them as people with hurts and pains and needs. When I would get on a plane I would pray, "Lord, I ask for the salvation of each of those on this plane." You see, it occurred to me that perhaps no one had ever prayed for some of them.

God's Harvest Can Even Be Found on an Airplane

Mike and I were returning from a trip to Europe when I closed my eyes and started to intercede, "Lord of the harvest, is there someone on this plane who needs to know you?" I was tired, the plane was packed, and we were sitting in economy. I felt like I had right to sit back. Yet, I felt a stirring in my heart as I prayed.

What should I do? I pondered. *Where could I find this harvest?* All of a sudden, with a stroke of what I later found out to be godly inspiration, I knew—I could meet someone by the restroom!

I quickly got up and went and got in a line of those waiting; all the while looking around and asking the Lord, "How can I connect with someone who is ready to know you?"

It wasn't long before a lovely lady with bright blue eyes who appeared to be in her late 60s or early 70s came up behind me and got in line. I turned to her and struck up a conversation about her trip. She asked, "Why were you in Europe?" I responded, "I am a minister; I write Christian books, and I was in Europe speaking, as was my husband."

"How interesting," she replied, "I recently checked a book out of my library on the power of prayer. It was fascinating and told of case studies where people of different religions had prayed for people in the hospital to be healed. The people were not aware that they were being prayed for, and so it was a blind test. Those who received prayer improved markedly over those who did not. Do you know anything about that kind of thing?"

Right then I knew that God had arranged this divine encounter. I looked around and saw that the restroom on my side had opened. I was next in line, so I smiled at her and said, "Tina [not her real name], I'll meet you out here in just a little bit. Don't go away." Her sweet face lit up as she affirmed that that would work.

Later, as we shared heart to heart, I could sense the Holy Spirit at work. Inwardly I was praying, *Lord, give me word of knowledge for her.* At that moment I received from the Lord that she was Jewish. I said to her, "Tina, are you Jewish?" She said, "Why yes, I am!"

That led into me sharing how I had been praying right before I met her and asked God if there was anyone I should meet on the plane who needed to know more about God. Her face lit up and she said, "Well, that is interesting because I was sitting in my seat praying to God in my own way, too!"

Of course, that was the perfect opening for me to share with her some Messianic passages from the Old Testament about Jesus Christ and before long, right in the aisle of the airplane, she prayed and asked Him into her life to be her Lord and Savior.

To say that I was happy would be a great understatement! I flew home the rest of the way with great rejoicing in my heart. There are people all around us who are hungry, desperate and who need a Savior. It is a matter of our praying and asking God to show us the keys to their heart. It might be a physical miracle, an act of kindness, or an offer of prayer. The point is that we need to be intentional in reaching out.

God Will Use You Wherever You Go

One of the most exciting, new and what I consider to be Jesus-people style applications of prophetic evangelism is the 24/7 movement out of England. Rebecca Jacob's daughter, Jasmine, gave me the story about 24/7, *Red Moon Rising*, while I was in Spain. It is called such because of the red moon symbolized in the book of Joel, and that is the way it looks during harvest (see Joel 2:31).

As a young man, Pete Greig, the coauthor of *Red Moon Rising*, was deeply affected by God when he was traveling across Europe with his friend Nick. One night as the two were camping on the cliffs of Cape St. Vincent, God gave Pete an astounding vision. They had pitched their tent on the absolute southwesterly point of Europe. Cape St. Vincent was the end of the world to the Romans and the place where monks had brought the body of St. Vincent, the martyr, to be laid to rest. Legend goes on to say that ravens guarded his body.

One night while his friend slept, Pete climbed out of the tent. Little did he know that God would give him a vision that night that would help change the world. This is how he described what he saw:

A breathtaking sight had greeted me; the vast, glowering ocean glimmering under a shimmering eternity of stars . . . to the south, the next great landmass is Africa. To the west, it is America. Visualizing nation after nation, I raised my hands and began to pray out loud for each one by name. And that was when it happened. First my scalp began to tingle and an electric current pulsed down my spine, again and again, physically shaking my body. I could hear a buzzing, clicking sound overhead, as if an electric pylon was short-circuiting, and I seriously wondered if I was about to get fried. As these strange sensations continued, I received a vision. My eyes were open, but I could "see" with absolute clarity before me the different countries laid out like an atlas. From each one a faceless army of young people rose from the page, crowds of them in every nation awaiting orders.[4]

This vision was later fulfilled in an incredible 24/7 prayer and evangelism movement birthed out of England. One of the chapters of *Red Moon Rising* has the great title "Ladies and Gentlemen, Church Has Left the Building." It recounts the story of a then-21-year-old woman named Bex. Bex went on holiday in Cyprus. After her vacation, she sensed the Holy Spirit urging her to return to the island.

According to Greig, Bex went back the next year to target the party town of Ayia Napa. Napa is a club capital and, prior to the arrival of the 24/7 group, there had been escalating gang tension and violence even reported by the international media. They found a shop to rent, only to be thrown out on the street and accused of witchcraft. Kicked out and homeless, they resorted to an ancient monastery and began to pray.

Their strategy was to prayer walk, pray in clubs, and break-dance on beaches. Through an amazing series of events, they ended up being invited to break-dance and to preach for two minutes at a beach party. The party included such things as sex games and drinking. However, the Holy Spirit was about to hijack the meeting.

After the break-dancing that was pretty popular, a young, blond prayer warrior got up to speak and was cursed by a group of girls while a group of guys started yelling, "Go for it!" The rest of the night was spent talking and praying with people about God and the young prayer warrior was invited back to preach to the group.[5]

It has been said that you should never discuss politics and religion with strangers. However, God doesn't look upon lost sheep of the world as strangers but rather as His created children that He is longing to show the Father's love. The 24/7 movement has learned how to demonstrate that in a tangible way.

You Can Feed the Poor and Take Care of the Needy

Part of that demonstration is through feeding the poor and taking care of the needy. As you ask God to show you the harvest, prophetic evangelism, through taking care of the needs of those who are suffering financially, will send a powerful message to a hurting generation.

Not long ago, my daughter, Madison, called me. She was beside herself with excitement. "Mom," she exclaimed, "I heard the voice of God today!" She went on to say that she had watched out of her window as two young Hispanic women got out of their car with little children and went to the garage sale next door.

The Holy Spirit spoke to her and said, "I want you to give them something." She couldn't imagine what that could be as she was low on money herself, so she knew it couldn't be monetary.

As she started walking around her house praying, the Lord spoke to her, "Give them your other car seat." She then remembered that none of the children had been using a car seat. "Lord," Madison returned, "I don't even know where that car seat is and our garage is full." Just then she stepped into her living room and, to her surprise, she saw the car seat sitting on the floor!

Madison quickly grabbed the car seat and ran outside before the women left and said to them, "This is for you!" They were quite surprised at this stranger's running out of her house and thrusting the child-protective seat into their hands. Madison then turned around and, with a cheery "God bless you!", scurried back into her house. The women were deeply touched by her gift. I am sure that we will see those women in heaven.

How Does God Want to Use You in Prophetic Evangelism?

Whether praying for a horse, break-dancing on a beach, or giving away a child's car seat, the Lord knows just the thing that will bring an individual closer to the kingdom of God.

Here are some specific tips on how to flow in prophetic evangelism:

1. Ask the Lord each day to direct you to the person(s) who is(are) ready to be harvested.

2. Always stay sensitive to the Holy Spirit's prompting as you go about your life.

3. Don't be afraid to go in the direction of that nudge, even if where it leads, at times, may seem foolish to you.

4. After you receive a word and deliver it, be prepared to lead the person to the Lord.

5. You may feel intimidated thinking that you may offend people if you ask them to pray with you to receive Christ. They will feel more offended in hell.

If you have never led anyone to the Lord, here are some Scriptures:

For God so loved the world that He gave His only begotten Son, that whoever believes in Him should not perish but have everlasting life (John 3:16).

For all have sinned and fall short of the glory of God (Rom. 3:23).

If you confess with your mouth the Lord Jesus and believe in your heart that God has raised him from the dead, *you will be saved* (Rom. 10:9, emphasis added).

Your Holy Spirit Adventures

What is the harvest? What are your harvest fields? Name specific places and people that God has given you. Now, what are you going to do to harvest the fields God has placed before you?

Has God ever used you in prophetic evangelism? Recount at least one time (particularly if it was during an encounter with a stranger). If this has never happened, you can pray right now that God will release this gifting in you as He did in Ché Ahn, Smith Wigglesworth, Bex and Madison. After God answers this prayer, come back to this journaling section and record what happened.

THE
ENTERTAINING
OF ANGELS

Leslyn Musch and I had just arrived in Caracas, Venezuela. As we stepped out of the airplane and into muggy night air, I said, "I sure hope that someone is here to pick us up. My Spanish is not very good." I was joking, but I was more prophetic than I knew.

It was around 9:30 P.M. and we were tired from a long day of travel. We collected our bags and headed through customs without any hassles. The doors whooshed open and we wheeled our luggage into a waiting area. Expectantly, we panned the crowd for some kind of welcoming sign or someone sent by the church to pick us up. There was no sign, nor was there a driver. We gave each other a maybe-they're-just-caught-in-traffic look.

The clock was ticking, so I decided to try out my Spanish. But everyone was leaving. To our consternation every shop started to close: the money exchange and ticket counters—everything. It happened so quickly that we didn't realize our predicament until it was too late.

We found some people and asked in our limited way if it was safe to go into the city via taxi. The people looked positively horrified and exclaimed, "*Peligro!*" That means "danger," and I understood that much. At last, after dragging our bags through more of the airport, we sat down in a conspicuous place. I poked my head outside to see if there were lines or traffic that would cause a delay, or if there was someone approaching who would say with relief (both theirs and ours), "I'm sorry to be late!" There was neither traffic nor a person looking for us. Leslyn and I sat down on our bags and looked at each other. I said to her, "I think it's time to pray—hard!" She agreed.

It got later and later and our prayers became more fervent when a nice looking, young, Venezuelan-appearing man wearing a suit approached us. "Hello," he cheerfully stated in perfect English, "I am here to meet VIPs. Do you need some help?"

His question was an understatement. Boy did we need help!

I had tried to phone the hotel earlier but learned that we needed a phone card; to acquire a phone card, we needed local currency—and the exchange was *cerado* (closed). I explained to the young man that we needed to call the hotel but didn't have a phone card. "No problem," he said, grinning and holding one up in the air. "I have one."

"Wonderful," I replied, and we walked around the corner to the phones, leaving Leslyn to guard the suitcases. I gave the young Venezuelan the number of the hotel and he dialed it, talked to the front desk and then handed the phone to me. Thankfully, the man on the other end of the line spoke English.

At last, we were getting somewhere, I thought with relief. While I waited for the hotel staffer to find our reservation I glanced over at the man in the airport and thanked the Lord for him. He gave me another of those wonderful grins and said, "By the way, my name is Luis, and I am angel from God." I stared at him blankly in unbelief as I held the receiver of the phone. "You are an angel?" Once again the big smile and then he pointed toward heaven and replied, "Yes, you know, from there."

Before I hung up the phone, arrangements had been made for a driver from the hotel to come pick us up. Luis and I walked back to Leslyn. I have to admit, I was in a bit of a state of shock. The fact that I had been helped by a real angel, sent by God, had not yet fully sunk in.

I told Leslyn that a car was coming to pick us up and when I turned around, Luis was gone. We never saw him again. The next day we found out that we had been expected at *10:00 A.M.* rather than *10:00 P.M.* That explained why there was no driver waiting for us. Thank God for our welcoming angel!

Do not forget to entertain strangers, for by so doing some have unwittingly entertained angels (Heb. 13:2).

What Makes Angels Angelic?

Most believers either have an angel story, or they can relate an incident where they were supernaturally protected. Whenever I speak on this subject and ask, "How many of you could tell me of a time when you were protected by what you felt was angelic intervention?" Most of the people in the audience will put their hands up.

The Bible is full of angel stories and even tells us that God sends angels to minister to us.

This is not surprising because the Bible is full of angel stories and even tells us that God sends them to minister to us (see Heb. 1:14).

Angels Deserve More Credit

In recent years, I, among others, have spoken and written on the subject of spiritual warfare. An integral portion of this kind of instruction needs to include teaching on angels. Around ten years ago I felt a need to make sure that I balanced the truth of fighting powers of darkness with that of an understanding of the power of God expressed through angelic forces.

I agree with Billy Graham, who wrote:

We must not get so busy counting demons that we forget the holy angels. Certainly we are up against a gigantic war machine. But we are encompassed by a heavenly host so powerful that we need not fear the warfare—the battle is the Lord's.[1]

I find it peculiar that in the church you can make mention of a possible demonic attack and no one blinks an eye; yet, you report the presence of an angel and many disbelieve. This response is even more amazing because the Bible teaches us that there are two active angels to one fallen angel (see Rev. 12:4). The truth is that angels are everywhere. You might even have entertained one yourself. One might have even have saved your life. Billy Graham recounted one such story:

A celebrated Philadelphia neurologist had gone to bed after an exceptionally tiring day. Suddenly he was awakened by someone knocking on his door. Opening it he found a little girl, poorly dressed and deeply upset. She told him her mother was very sick and asked him if he would please come with her. It was a bitterly cold, snowy night, but though he was bone tired, the doctor dressed and followed the girl.

As the *Reader's Digest* reports the story, he found the mother desperately ill with pneumonia. After arranging for medical care, he complimented the sick woman on the intelligence and persistence of her little daughter. The woman looked at him strangely and then said, "My daughter died a month ago." She added, "Her shoes and coat are in the clothes closet there." Amazed and perplexed, the doctor went to the closet and opened the door. There hung the very coat worn by the little girl who had brought him to tend to her mother. It was dry and warm and could not possibly have been out in the wintry night.

Could the doctor have been called in the hour of desperate need by an angel who appeared as this woman's young daughter? Was this the work of God's angels on behalf of the sick woman?[2]

Angels Appear Everywhere

The Bible records 104 appearances of angels to humankind. Angels are mentioned 52 times in the book of Revelation alone. This is enough to give us quite a broad picture about these wondrous creations of God. I looked into Scripture to become better acquainted with those the Bible defines as "encamped around us" (Ps. 34:7). Here are some facts that I've gleaned:

- Angels cannot be numbered (see Heb. 12:22). This is comforting! The angels are all around you, ministering to you and guarding you.
- Angels speak in an angelic language, yet they also speak in earthly languages (see 1 Cor. 13:1). The Angel of the Lord appeared to Abraham and spoke in Abraham's native tongue. Perhaps the angel spoke to Hagar in her native tongue, too.
- Angels have been known to provide people with food and water (see 1 Kings 19:5-7). An angel appeared to Elijah the Tishbite when he was running from Jezebel. When Elijah was exhausted and hungry, he was fed by the angel.
- Angels have emotions. The Bible records that they have great joy when one sinner repents (see Luke 15:10).

- Angels can appear in a visible manner and have spiritual bodies that can be seen (see Gen. 18:2,4,8; Num. 22:22-23,31.) This explains why Leslyn and I could see Luis.
- While angels may not need to eat, they can do so—Abraham fed them butter, milk and a calf (see Gen. 18:8).
- Angels are immortal (see Luke 20:36).
- Angels are not to be worshiped (see Col. 2:18).
- Animals can see angels (see Num. 22:22-23).
- Angels move quickly, perhaps at the speed of light (see Ezek. 1:14).
- Angels do not marry (see Mark 12:25).
- There are different orders of angelic beings (see Deut. 32:8).

God Gives the Angels Territorial Assignments

Early Church leader Clement of Alexandria said, "The presiding powers of the angels have been distributed according to the nations and the cities."[3] Clement's conclusion could be expanded to include angels being distributed over churches and this has biblical moorings:

The mystery of the seven stars which you saw in My right hand, and the seven golden lampstands: The seven stars are the angels of the seven churches, and the seven lampstands which you saw are the seven churches (Rev. 1:20).

Pastors often teach that this passage addresses the angels who watch over the churches. Could it also be addressing humans? There were human overseers and angels also assigned to the individual churches. Since Satan is the great counterfeiter, it is possible he observed the human-angelic overseer pattern in the Church and in nations and copied it with his wicked angels.

The highly respected Early Church writer Pseudo-Dionysius concluded:

> If the nations have their good angels sent by God to assist and guide them, they are also the prey of demons who turn them away from the true God. Thus, demons take the place of the angels in the government and directions of nations and, thus, there is question of evil angels more frequently than of good angels.[4]

I have heard many people describe what they have seen in visions concerning principalities over nations. However, not enough has been said or written about angels over nations. Yet, their existence makes sense; as Pseudo-Dionysius concluded, it makes sense that since Satan is not capable of creating anything and can only counterfeit them, demons mimic and try to take over the role of chief angel over each nation. In Bible days, the word "nation" applied to clans and people groups. Today, we apply that concept to the relatively recent creation of nation-states. Either way, there is a monumental spiritual struggle going on right now over every nation. In this case, it would mean that each nation has its own chief angel. This could lead to the conclusion that there is a ruling angel assigned to the United States, one for Finland, another for Chile, and so forth.

Why aren't these angels seen more often? I have a theory. There cannot be two ruling entities over a nation. Depending upon our intercession, the righteousness or sin of a nation, and other spiritual factors, either the angel of the Lord or a fallen angel will be enthroned over that country.

There Is an Angel in My Living Room

My journey into the subject of angels presiding over nations began in 1984. One night around 10:30 P.M., I was drying dishes. At that time, we lived in Weatherford, Texas. Our house was designed so that I could look from the kitchen, through the dining room and into the living room.

As I worked, it seemed to me that I could feel an unusual presence of God emanating from the living room. With a dishtowel in my hand, I stood for a few moments in wonder. At last I started walking toward the living room.

As this angel gazed at me, it was as if I were enveloped by liquid love, acceptance, peace, joy and reverent fear all at once.

When my feet touched the carpet of the room, in amazement I gazed at a glorious angel. He was sitting in a tall, winged-back blue velvet chair, and he was enormous! His shoulders went at least a foot or more over the top of the high-backed chair. I had noted that the angels in Scripture are all dressed in white—this angel wore a robe of that color, a sash of gold and sandals on his feet. The most unusual feature of his dress was a thin gold crown that went across his forehead. His hair was light brown, shoulder-length and parted in the middle.

The most riveting thing about him were his eyes. What eyes! It is almost impossible to describe them. I can't even recall a specific color, but they pierced me to the bottom of my soul. As this angel gazed at me, it was as if I were enveloped by liquid love, acceptance, peace, joy and reverent fear all at once. At that moment, I knew why each angel noted in the Bible would say to those they visited, "Fear not!"

It was as if this angel in my living room knew all my failings yet loved me without condemnation. I fell to my face on the floor, my dishtowel still in hand. Out of my mouth came the words "It's the Lord!" He replied to me, "I am the Angel of the Lord, stand on your feet!"

Slowly I stood to listen to the message that this angel brought. While I cannot express in words all that he said, his visit triggered more.

God Speaks Through a Vision

Soon after the angel visited my living room in Weatherford, Texas, the Lord God touched my life in many great ways. One significant turning point came when I had a vision of the finger of God outlining South America in fire beginning with Colombia and continuing until the whole continent burst into flames before my eyes.

After the vision, God spoke to my heart and said, "I am going to use you to help touch this whole continent for the gospel."

How could this happen? I pondered. At the time, I was just barely beginning to travel in ministry. However, God has His ways of advertising.

I Go to Argentina

Through a series of divine encounters, my husband, Mike, and I met Peter and Doris Wagner, who were friends with our now good friend Ed Silvoso, the leader of Harvest Evangelism.

The first time I went to Argentina, I was relatively unknown in the ministry, but not unknown to God. Silvoso's Harvest team arranged for a small advertisement to be put in the newspaper announcing that I was coming to teach on intercession. To their surprise (and mine, too), ministers flew in from across the nation.

Abraham Had Seen an Angel

One of those in attendance was a young indigenous man named Abraham. A few years earlier, he had had a rather dramatic encounter with God and had been born again. An angel had appeared to him upright in a 30-foot-high pillar of fire. This angel showed Abraham a vision of a woman who would come to Argentina and help bring revival to the nation. Part of his instruction was to tell the pastors that I was coming.

Abraham was obedient and went by bus from pastor's office to pastor's office. When I stood to speak, those he visited had been given a description of me. That description matched the person who they now saw in the flesh, and they realized that I had been sent by the Lord. Never doubt that God is able to open doors that no man can shut (see Isa. 22:22).

I Was Not the Only One Visited by the Angel

The next year, I returned to Argentina. As I stood to teach in a hotel in Mar del Plata, I thought of the angel who had visited me in my living room. There were around 1,000 pastors and leaders in the ballroom that day. I was 37, almost 38 years old.

I told the pastors about my living-room encounter and the message I had received. I also described the angel. During the break between sessions, a local pastor approached me to tell me that he had a vision of the same angel with the golden crown on his forehead the same year that

I had. The message the angel brought was the same: "There is a great revival coming to South America."

When the meeting resumed, I called the pastor forward and asked him to share his testimony. It was like a bomb had been dropped in our midst. Leaders began to drop to their knees and fell on the floor prostrate. Weeping could be heard across the room. An angelic presence filled the room as a great amen resounded from each heart. It was as if in unison, we all shouted, "Lord, do it! Bring a sweeping revival to this nation and to all of South America." Since that day souls have been saved and churches have grown from Buenos Aires to Bogotá to Rio de Janeiro.

On another trip, I shared this story in Bogotá, at what became the fastest growing church in the world. I posed the question: "Has anyone seen an angel of this description?" Three young women stepped forward—none of them knew each other. They each said the angel that they saw was similar with a small difference. The difference was that the one that appeared to them had emeralds set in the crown of the forehead. Could it be that they saw the angel of the Lord over Colombia and he wears the emeralds representing the nation over which he is stationed? (Colombia is known for its beautiful emeralds.)

Through the years I have had visions of the angel of the Lord over certain nations just prior to a great revival coming to that nation. Perhaps they have come in answer to the cries of Christians who wanted to see God move in those nations.

An Angel Comes after September 11

The weekend after the tragic September 11, 2001, attacks on America, Generals of Intercession, the ministry Mike and I lead, was scheduled to hold a prayer conference in Boise, Idaho. Everyone was still reeling from the events of the preceding week and praying and weeping before the Lord together, as were thousands of other Christians around the world. Dutch Sheets, our pastor when we lived in Colorado Springs, was at the conference. As he led the group in prayer for our nation, I saw an amazing sight.

Standing behind Dutch on the platform, at least twenty feet in height, stood an angel. I knew that this was the angel of the Lord over America.

Standing behind Dutch on the platform, at least twenty feet in height, stood an angel. I knew that this was the angel of the Lord over America. The angel wore a crown like that which is on the statue of liberty and held a torch in his hand. Across his shoulders, like a mantle, was draped an American flag. As Dutch prayed and prophesied over the nation, there was a corresponding action from the angel. When Dutch cried, "Wind of God, blow across this land," the angel would fill his cheeks with wind and blow the power of the Holy Spirit on the states receiving the prophecy.

Dutch went on to say, "Fire of God, fall! Fall on Idaho, fall on Washington, D.C., fall on California." At this the angel extended his torch and the fire of God came out from it and extended across the particular state receiving the Word of the Lord. It was as if the two of them were working in tandem, the intercession of heaven and Earth pouring out of the church into the nation.

God Has His Hand on Russia, Too

In 2001, some friends and I took a prayer journey to Russia. One day in St. Petersburg, we prayed to break the strongholds that Grigory Rasputin (a Siberian mystic who arrived in St. Petersburg in 1911) had put upon the land. After we prayed, we went to a hotel for the night. As I was attempting to fall asleep, it was as if the heavens opened up and I saw a great angel come down with keys in his hands. The angel was so unusual looking to my Western thinking that I wasn't sure that what I was seeing was real.

The angel was dressed in robes of ermine and had a crown upon his head in what looked like dark mink. He had a cross on the top of the crown. The portion of the vision that I questioned was the fact that he wore a long beard. I had never seen nor heard of an angel with a beard. Nonetheless, he took the keys and began unlocking the treasures of the nation. First he went to the hermitage and then all through the city of St. Petersburg.

God is faithful to confirm visions when they are from Him. Later that week we were touring the armory in Moscow where the Czar's jewels and possessions are displayed. We came to the section where the attire and crown of the first Czar was displayed. To my amazement the robes looked exactly as I had seen in the vision and the crown matched also!

Of course, I realize that this is all subjective; but couldn't this be said of all visions? I earnestly believe this was a sign from the Lord that all the territory once ruled over by the Czars will see a great and mighty move of God.

God Calls Some Angels by Name

Some commentaries suggest that the seven angels who stand before God (see Rev. 8:2) are chief princes or archangels, and that God even takes counsel from them. Is it possible that each one would represent a continent?

While the Bible does not reveal much about these chief princes or archangels, writing found in the apocrypha and book of Enoch do explain more about them. According to the apocrypha (see Tobit 12:15), Raphael is one of the seven holy angels who stand before God.

Michael is the only angel who is actually given the title of a chief prince in Scripture (see Dan. 10:13; Jude 9). He is called the great prince who is the special guardian of the Jews. Often described as the warrior angel, we know of Michael primarily from the Scripture passage where he fought against the prince of Persia to get the message of God to Daniel.

Another chief prince is Gabriel, the heavenly messenger. He was sent to Daniel to explain to him the vision of God (see Dan. 8:16; 9:21). Gabriel also announced the birth of John the Baptist to his father, Zacharias (see Luke 1:11), and of the Lord Jesus to the Virgin Mary (see Luke 1:16).

God Will Establish a Great Company of Women
In 1999, I was in the city of Barcelona, Spain, with my friend Julie Anderson. We were staying at an old, high-ceilinged hotel. After an excellent dinner in that beautiful city, we retired for the night. Around three A.M., I was awakened by a voice, "Wake up! I want to talk with you! I am Gabriel and I am here to give you a message from God." I did not see him; nonetheless, I had no doubt that he was who he said he was.

The next thing I knew, I was having a vision of mounting and riding a huge chestnut horse and my friend Julie was mounting and riding a white stallion. She was part of a vast army of women. As the Lord showed me country after country, I saw thousands of women on horseback behind me to march across the earth. In the vision, I was wearing armor and carried a sword. I must admit that my first thought not very spiritual. I thought, *I could never wear armor like this, nor lift this sword. I'd fall off the horse from the weight.* I heard a chuckle and snapped back into a more spiritual state. Gabriel said, "I assure you, God will help you wear this for the battle."

Gabriel told me that the women in vision comprised a great company of women who would march across the planet, preaching the gospel, doing miracles, and transforming the nations. These women were to be a Deborah Company and I was to help find them and release them. This is much like what we read in Psalm 68:11. In fact, many translations do not clearly denote that the Hebrew word used for "company" in this verse is both feminine and plural—thus, a great company of women.

Since that day God has helped me as I have endeavored to do just what the heavenly vision mandated. The Lord has shown me that there are women, both young and old, who will change the nations of the earth through following the call of God on their lives. (Men are important, too; but this vision was to show me my responsibility in helping to raise up women leaders.)

God Created Different Types of Angels

Two other unique orders of angels are the cherubim and seraphim. These are both winged angels, though not all angels are winged.

The first biblical account of cherubim was when they were sent by God to guard the Garden of Eden with a flaming sword so that Adam and Eve could not reenter after the Fall.

Psalm 18:19 reveals that God rides upon a cherub. It may be that God does His will through the cherubim and thus "rides" upon them.

This gives a different picture from the little baby cherubim that we often see in artwork.

The four beasts noted in Revelation 4:6 that have the face of a man in front, the face of a lion on the right, the face of an ox on the left, and the face of an eagle on the back are cherubim. They have hands like a man under their wings on their four sides and four wings. Their feet are like those of calves. In appearance they look like burning coats of fire and lamps, and they run and return like flashes of lightning (see Ezek. 1:4-14).

Angels Love to Be Around People Who Worship God
According to *Nelson's Bible Dictionary*, angels are often associated with worship and praise of God. The Ark of the Covenant had two cherubim, each with a wingspan of 15 feet. They are glorious and wondrous beings. Some commentators feel they are connected with vindicating the holiness of God against man's presumptuous sin.

Seraphim Burn with Fire
Seraphim are the order of celestial beings that Isaiah saw in Isaiah 6:2,6. The Hebrew word "seraph" actually means "burning" or "fiery." Picture with me these amazing creations of God, as described in this passage, as having six wings. With two they cover their face (perhaps as a show of humility before God), two others cover their feet (a show of respect), and with two they fly.

According to Isaiah, angels fly with a hot coal touching the lips of the prophet, purging his sin. Judging from their cry of "Holy, holy, holy," and their celebration of His holiness, they could likely be demanding a purging of God's people. A number of years ago I was studying about these magnificent creations and said out loud, "Oh, how I would love to see a seraphim!" At that moment, the room started to fill with the glory of God and my face felt tremendous heat. I cried, "Oh, I am not ready, Lord!" Immediately there was a receding of the presence and I determined I needed to do some heart searching and personal housecleaning.

Some Angels Are Destroyers

One rank of these creations that is rarely talked about is the destroying angels. I believe from reading biblical accounts that we have no idea how immense the power of God's angels is. As I read accounts of angels bringing incredible destruction, it made me wonder why anyone would dare mock God; and it made me appreciate even more that His mercy is upon those whom He is calling to Himself. Genesis 19:12-13 provides one example:

> Then the men (angels) said to Lot, "Have you anyone else here? Son-in-law, your sons, your daughters, and whomever you have in the city—take them out of this place! For we will destroy this place, because the outcry against them has grown great before the face of the Lord, and the Lord has sent us to destroy it.

The mighty army of Assyria was destroyed by God.

> He shall not come into this city, Nor shoot an arrow there, Nor come before it with shield . . . By the way that he came, By the way shall he return. "For I will defend this city, to save it for my own sake and for My servant David's sake." And it came to pass on a certain

night that the angel of the Lord went out, and killed in the camp of the Assyrians one hundred and eighty-five thousand; and when people arose early in the morning, there were the corpses—all dead. So Sennacherib king of Assyria departed and went away, returned home, and remained at Nineveh (2 Kings 19:32-36).

Everyone Needs a Guardian Angel

Isn't it comforting to think that while angels are able to destroy whole cities, God still sends orders of them to protect and take care of us? One of these orders that we most believe in, even though there isn't as much biblical substance, is that of guardian angels.

There are two main passages that note the existence of guardian angels. One of these is Matthew 18:10:

Take heed that you do not despise one of these little ones, for I say to you that in heaven their angels always see the face of My Father who is in heaven.

The other passage is Acts 12:13-15:

And as Peter knocked at the door of the gate, a girl named Rhoda came to answer. When she recognized Peter's voice, because of her gladness she did not open the gate, but ran in and announced that Peter stood before the gate. But they said to her, "You are beside yourself!" Yet she kept insisting that it was so. So they said, "It is his angels."

In his commentary on the book of Acts, Peter Wagner writes:

The idea that people, especially children, have guardian angels is so prevalent that many assume it is something explicitly taught in the Bible. . . . The Jerusalem believers exclaiming **"It is his angel"** is about as close as any biblical passage comes. . . . All we do know from this is that the concept that Peter might have **his angel** was common then, as it is among many today.[5] (Emphasis is Wagner's.)

I personally do not find it farfetched to think that each of us has a guardian angel to protect us. One day I was driving in Texas on a two-lane road when suddenly there was a big 18-wheeler truck right in front of me in my lane. All I remember is crying out to God for protection. The next thing I knew was that the truck was behind me and I was safe and sound. How did that happen? It had to be angels.

Angels not only protect individuals, but they also protect nations in time of war. Billy Graham used this illustration:

In the early days of World War II, Britain's air force saved it from invasion and defeat. In her book, *Tell No Man*, Adela Rogers St. John describes a strong aspect of that week-long air war. Her information comes from a celebration held some months after the war, honoring Air Chief Marshal Lord Hugh Dowding. The king, the prime minister and scores of dignitaries were there. In his remarks the air chief marshal recounted the story of his legendary conflict where his pitifully small complement of men rarely slept, and their planes never stopped flying. He told about airmen on a mission who were either incapacitated or dead. Yet their planes kept flying and flying; in fact, on occasion pilots in other planes would see a figure still operating the controls. What was the explanation? The air chief marshal said he believed angels had actually flown some of the planes whose pilots sat dead in their cockpits.[6]

Have You Ever Met an Angel?

I'm sure that you have entertained angels whether you are aware of it or not. As a college student, I would often drive home to the dormitory around 11:45 P.M. Many nights I noticed a short, sweet little lady carrying a few bundles at different places around my part of the city. One day she would be on one street, and then another far away. Curiosity got the best of me and, late one night, I stopped to ask her if I could give her a ride somewhere. She looked at me and, with a lovely musical voice, said, "Oh, no thank you, honey. My Lord will be around to get me shortly." I never saw her again after that.

Maybe the Father just wanted to know if I would care for a little old woman. I don't really know. I do know that I drove away with a sense of awe from that one little stop in my life that has never left my heart.

Whole books have been written on the subject of angels. These wonderful supernatural beings are all around you. It is good to remember the admonition that Elisha the prophet gave in 2 Kings 6:16: "Do not fear, for those who are with us are many more than those who are with them." You are never alone and the angels of God are working, protecting and intervening in your life's circumstances at this very moment.

Your Holy Spirit Adventures

Have you ever seen an angel. Recount your experience. Why do you think God sent this angel your way?

Have you ever sensed the presence of an angel or been protected by an angel. Put what you felt into words. What do you think about God having a guardian angel assigned to you?

SUPERNATURAL ADVENTURES

I have never before told some of the stories that I now include in this chapter. I feel that God has given me a focus on intercession and the prophetic, but during this season I feel that I should redirect the spotlight toward the miraculous and book of Acts experiences. One of the most exciting aspects of the supernatural is the fact that we, as believers, can have adventures in the Holy Spirit that reveal to those around us the supernatural nature of God. In this chapter, I recount story after story to encourage you in your journey.

You Will Do Greater Things

In coming days, many of you are going to flow in the aspect of not only signs, but also great and mighty wonders. With this in mind, the instruction and testimonies in this chapter will cause faith to rise up in your heart. You will be stirred to do even greater things *than I and others have accomplished through the name of Jesus.*

God often works this way—doing greater things as each new generation comes along. In the middle part of the 20th century, Kathryn Kuhlman had a remarkable healing ministry. At her funeral in 1976, evangelist Oral Roberts received a tremendous vision about greater things to come. The vision was that God would raise up and spread similar ministries throughout the world, making the magnitude of God's power greater than He had done through Kathryn's life.[1]

In this book you have been introduced to many great men and women of God, such as Kathryn Kuhlman. (These and others have been my teachers in the supernatural. This in no way discounts the Holy Spirit Himself. He, of course, was, and is, the ever-present and ultimate instructor.) During the late 1970s and 1980s, I would pour over book after book written about these great men and women of faith.

As I have already noted, as I read I would pray and say, "Lord, I want to do these things and greater." Often I would get down on my knees and weep as I cried out to the Lord for revival and the harvest in the nations. At times I wrote notes in the margins that read something like:

Father God, according to Mark 11:24, whatever things I ask in prayer You will give them to me. Right now, I am asking for the miracles I've read about on these pages and more to be manifest as I pray for the sick.

I would also read through the book of Acts, time and again, and believe that in my life I would see every type of miracle and wonder recorded there. Those prayers have been answered. I have been translated (like Philip), seen the blind see, witnessed the lame walk, observed the dead raised, and so much more.

Wonders prompt the fear of God and the reality that He is real to pour into your soul.

I know that the Bible is the Manufacturer's handbook. God has written precise instructions on what you can expect if you follow them exactly. At times people make things too complicated rather than simply believing what God has said. I took God at His word. I expected Him not only to do the regular miracles, such as healing headaches, but I also anticipated wonders.

Wonders Are Wondrous

One aspect of supernatural ministry that has not often been singled out for examination is that of wonders. The Bible declares that in the last days, God will show wonders in the heavens and on Earth—this will include blood, fire and pillars of smoke.

What are wonders? They are supernatural experiences that make you wonder at the marvelous power of God. In fact, in some Scriptures the word "wondrous" is translated "marvelous." Wonders prompt the fear of God and the reality that He is real to pour into your soul as you watch or hear about the power of God. Acts 2:43 declares that great fear came upon every soul and many wonders and signs were done through the apostles.

God Overcame Time and Distance

Many of the wonders I have seen stretch the imagination. For example, I read about Philip being "caught away" (see Acts 1:40), but it was altogether amazing to actually be translated from one place to another. By being translated, I mean that God moved me through time and space. Let me explain.

As I studied Acts, I noticed a small, but intriguing passage. Philip had been instructed by the Holy Spirit to go from Jerusalem to Gaza. There he met an Ethiopian man who was the treasurer of the queen of the Ethiopians. The man was reading the book of Isaiah.

The Lord told Philip to overtake the chariot (this was perhaps a miracle in and of itself!). Philip witnessed to the Ethiopian and baptized him, then he was "caught away" and the Eunuch saw him no more. The next thing Philip knew, he was in Azotus (see Acts 1:39-40). Imagine this amazing scene! One minute Philip is on the road to Gaza, the next moment he is in a city 30 or so miles away. Now that is a wonder!

After reading this interesting account, I prayed, *Lord, you know that I often drive long hours. I would really appreciate it if you would shave some time off of them for me.*

One day it happened. I was driving from Forth Worth, Texas, to Temple, Texas, where I was to speak. All I recall is seeing the Fort Worth sign and then in the blink of an eye, I looked up and I was almost there. I looked down at the clock and noted that five minutes had passed; yet I had covered more than 90 miles.

This has since happened a number of times. You would think that God would translate someone only when there was a pressing ministry need (seems that Philip needed to get to the next place where people needed to hear the Good News), but sometimes my entire family has been translated. One time when my daughter was younger, she was tired and dreaded a long ride in a car. Knowing what had happened to me on my way to Waco, she prayed that God would get the entire family to our destination—fast! God amazed even me when He answered my little girl's prayer and we were translated (the trip took an hour less than it should have).

On another occasion, I was riding in a car with a friend on my way to a speaking engagement and I briefly recounted how God previously had translated me. My friend and I had noted the time before we left and when we arrived—only two minutes had passed on a trip that always took at least fifteen minutes or more! It had happened again.

Isn't that a wonder?

Curious, as anyone would be, I asked God, "Father, how are you doing this?" I think that I heard a chuckle and then a reply, "I'm just taking you in and out of time."

It is important to note that God does not take me in and out of time every time I need to get somewhere fast. Yes, I still get stuck in traffic jams and have to spend hours on the road. Moreover, I cannot snap my fingers and zip off to another place. Being translated only occurs when and where God wants it to occur. And usually when I least expect it.

Miracles Can Be Expected

You should expect to have supernatural adventures in your walk with God. You are His child and He is supernatural. The power of the Holy Spirit lives in you. The Bible promises you that you can do greater things because Jesus went to be with the Father (see John 14:12). Inside every believer lives the God who created the universe and everything in it. He is also the God who parted the Red Sea.

God Parts the Waters in Vietnam

Stories such as the parting of the Red Sea and my belief that I could do all the other things seen in Scripture, too, emboldened my faith during a prayer journey I took to Vietnam in 1997.

Seven of us were in DaNang City and we were praying. We felt that God had prompted us to go to Marble Mountain, which overlooks the old United States military base there. We were to break the curses the Buddhists had placed upon our servicemen and women during the Vietnamese War. A ministry specializing in ministry to Vietnam Vets had told us about these curses, some of which specified that the soldiers would be homeless and bear no fruit.

The morning we had planned to go and pray, the enemy fought against our plans. A maid woke up my friend Chuck Pierce at 5:30 A.M. and told him that floodwaters were rising and that we had better leave the city right away or we might not be able to get out. He promptly knocked on my door to tell me the news.

The gift of faith rose up in me and I asked for our team to gather. We went to the small balcony that overlooked the street to observe the situation. The streets were already flooded. People were actually traveling on them in boats! It didn't look like we would make it to Marble Mountain.

We found the passage in Exodus where Moses parted the Red Sea, raised our Bibles and commanded the river to stop flooding.

We had heard that the main problem was that the river was over-flowing because there had been large amounts of rainfall. However, I knew that God had told me that we were to go to that mountain on this particular day.

In a flash I had the understanding of how to fix the problem. We would stand on the balcony and command the water to part and stop flooding! Wow, the Holy Spirit is brilliant!

The rest of the team gave me one of those if-you-say-so-Cindy looks, and we proceeded. First we worshiped God. Don Hinton had become our team musician after he had purchased a little flute for around ten cents. He played as we stood on the balcony and sang, all the while waving to the people who were in the boats. Next we found the passage in Exodus where Moses parted the Red Sea (see Exod. 14:21-22), raised our Bibles and commanded the river to stop flooding and the streets to dry up. Within one hour the flooding, that was expected to take three days to dry out, had completely gone down. We loaded into a van and were on our way. God is indeed a God of wonders!

Like the song of Moses, we proceeded with the words from Exodus 15:11 in our hearts:

Who is like unto you, O Lord among the gods, who is like unto you, glorious in holiness, fearful in praises, *doing wonders* (emphasis added).

God parted the waters on that trip not once, but twice. As we were attempting to leave Vietnam, a monsoon rolled in, complete with enough rain to flood the runway at the airport. Our team looked at each with a laugh and said, "Well, time for the wonder-working God to do it again"— and of course He did!

You Need to Spend Time with God

Spending time with the Lord and seeking His face is an important aspect of supernatural adventures. There are moments when you are in prayer that God will carry you beyond the natural into the supernatural realm, or what the Bible calls being "caught up"—He might even give you heavenly visions (see 2 Cor. 12:2).

I Wear a Dress of Diamonds

Years ago I was going through a particularly difficult season in my life. It seemed that not everyone thought the spiritual warfare message was biblical. Moreover, not everyone welcomed a woman teaching that message—or any message, for that matter.

One day during worship I was caught up and it seemed like the heavens were opened to me and I stood in the throne room of God. I had on a luminous white gown that appeared to be made of thousands of twinkling diamonds. My first thought was rather worldly: *One cannot wear a dress made of diamonds, Lord!* I chuckled. I could tell that the Lord was indulging me when He said, "Cindy, you will understand that in heaven you can wear a garment of diamonds and it will be totally comfortable. The elements on the earth are only a shadow of what they are in heaven." That made sense.

Another thing I noted was that the gown felt perfectly comfortable. Usually in one zone of your body you will feel a binding from your clothes or will feel cooler or hotter from one part to the other. Not so in heaven! I had never felt so comfortable in my life! I was totally climate controlled.

It seemed the air was full of joy. The atmosphere literally sparkled with tiny little flashes of light that released the joy of the Lord. That day the Father ministered such peace to me. It is interesting to note that one day, years later, while sitting around our kitchen table with John and Paula Sandford, we exchanged Holy Spirit adventure stories about heaven. We were delighted to find that we had seen some of the same things!

God's People See Signs and Wonders

I am particularly excited about the youth that is rising up around the world today. Members of this young generation have great faith and believe God not only for signs but also for marvelous wonders. I call this the Joshua generation after Joshua of the Old Testament. It was Joshua who instructed the people to sanctify themselves and to expect the Lord to do wonders.

The Jesus People Knew How to Pray, Too
Bible teacher Dick Eastman records how God used the youth to help intercede for what we now know as the Jesus Movement during the early 1970s. During the end of the 1960s, Eastman and his wife, Dee, established what they called prayer corps that met in what they called firehouses. However, they wanted to start fires, not put them out. The record of the miracles that resulted is found in Eastman's book *The Purple Pig and other Miracles: Cripples Walk, Floods Are Stopped; the Sick Are Healed.*

One of the marvelous stories Eastman tells about this season of praying with youth is found in another of his books: *Dick Eastman on Prayer*. The prayer corps learned that Eastman meant business when it came to intercession. One night during the later part of the 1960s, he took a group of 22 participants to the mountains. Eastman wrote:

Not one of us, for instance, knew how to pray an entire night, and frankly we were all about to give up after less than an hour. Then the youngest participant, a thirteen-year old asked us to start praying in a different way—as warriors. He saw himself and his friends as warring against the darkness of the booze-sex-drugs lifestyle of the hippie communes, and he asked us to stand with him all night to "fight the devil." The youth had tears in his eyes as he spoke, and all agreed to go to war along with him.

By three in the morning a spirit of brokenness had settled over our retreat house. The room was warmly lit by a glow from logs burning in a large fireplace, but also from a fire burning within the young people themselves. We all began to weep and cry out. One seventeen-year-old student lay on her face in the middle of the room weeping for the youth of California who were in trouble with drugs.[2]

Eastman later told me that as he knelt down to listen to what the 17-year-old girl was praying, he heard her cry out for her generation with weeping and travail. God answered those prayers and those of others with a sweeping move of the Holy Spirit that was called the Jesus Movement.

It Is Important to Obey God's Voice
Eastman's faithfulness to have the students pray launched something beyond his wildest dreams. He has learned not only to listen to the voice of God, but also to do what He says!

Eastman makes the point that when you hear God, you must act upon what He says. If you obey His voice, then He will do wonders in your life (see Jer. 11:4-5). God gave this powerful command to Jeremiah.[3]

You might say, "Cindy, obeying God does involve a certain measure of risk." This observation reminds me of a sermon that my father (who was a preacher) once gave. I have his sermon notes on little 3-inch-by-5-inch cards. One card read, "Great people are willing to take big risks. Small people rarely do." When God speaks He expects you to believe Him largely and then you will see major wonders.

If you obey God's voice, then He will do wonders in your life.

God Told Guillermo to Buy a Synagogue and Land

A friend of mine from Miami, Guillermo Maldonado, knows about hearing and obeying. Years ago I called him out from a group of around 50 pastors who were attending a meeting in Miami, Florida. The word for him was, "Go buy a synagogue." This is certainly a specific and unusual word. There are not synagogues for sale on every street corner. However, Guillermo believed the prophecy and began to drive around his community looking for one.

When at last he found one, he made an offer. The only problem was that he had no money to put down—but he had the word. Taking a leap of faith based on the prophecy, he had to believe that God would provide a very large sum of money in a very short time. God met Guillermo in a big way, and the synagogue was purchased.

Guillermo came to me later and said, "Cindy, do you know the next thing God says for me to do?" I thought a moment and listened to the Holy Spirit and said, "Go and buy a large piece of property. You will know that it is yours because it will be by a major gateway to the city, have high-end homes at the end of it and an artificial lake."

This was a very specific, detailed word. He told me later that he drove around the city for seven months looking for that property. Finally he knew where to look. The regional airport is a gateway. He went to the airport and then walked across the street to an empty field. He walked to the back of field where he found high-end homes and the artificial lake— this was it!

Guillermo excitedly called the owner and asked him if he would sell the 38-acre parcel of land. The man said, "How much money do you have?" (Does this sound familiar?) Guillermo said, "None." The man said, "I don't know why I am doing this, but I am going to give you the contract." Once again, the wonder-working God came through for that congregation and they own the land today.

Poisened Waters Cannot Stop These Missionaries

Wonders circumvent natural laws. Elisha was a prophet of wonders. In one account, in 2 Kings 6:5-6, an axe head fell into the water; Elisha cut down a stick and threw it into the water and the axe head floated to the surface. I know that today is a day when not only prophets but also those who believe will see the Elisha anointing.

There are times when God does wonders in our midst without our even being aware of it. Peter and Doris Wagner were missionaries in Bolivia for sixteen years. During that time they would, at times, take journeys deep into the eastern Bolivian jungle. On one particular day, accompanied by their 4-year-old daughter, Karen, they decided to go by horseback to visit missionary friends. Once on their way, they noted that they had forgotten to bring water. "No problem," they shared with one another, "we'll simply drink from the pools of water along the way."

Later upon arriving at the village where their friends' lived, the missionary wife, Phoebe, asked, "Where are your canteens?" The missionaries paled when they heard that the Wagners had drunk from the pools along the way. It seems that the Ayore Indians that this couple worked with had poisoned the pools with a certain fruit. This was their customary way to fish. The Ayores would poison the water, the fish would float to the surface, and the Ayores would simply scoop up the fish and dry them for food. Yet the Wagners showed no effects from the poisoned waters.

What a mighty God we serve! God protected the Wagner family, even though they were unaware that they were drinking poisoned water. Mark 16:18 is still true today:

They will take up serpents, and if they drink anything deadly, it will by no means hurt them.

God's Oil Flows

Another biblical wonder that I have seen is the multiplying of oil. Years ago I was ministering in a hotel in Colorado Springs, Colorado. When it came time for ministry at the end of the service, I heard the Lord say, "Tonight I want you to anoint people in the Old Testament way." I knew what He meant. He wanted me to pour the oil on their heads rather than dab it on their foreheads.

"How should I do it?" I asked God, and sent someone for sheets and towels. Within a few moments a friend whizzed into the room with a maid's cart full of towels and sheets. We spread out the sheets and I held up a quart-sized bottle of extra virgin olive oil.

"Tonight we are going to see God do wonders and you are going to go home with a new fresh touch from Him," I announced.

The people in the room knelt down on the sheets and we put white towels around each person's shoulders. The only way I can describe what happened is to compare it to a fire that hit each person the moment the oil touched him or her. It seemed as if a cloud of glory filled the room.

A crowd of people stood around and looked on in awe. I thought it was simply because of the way God was moving in the lives of those for whom we prayed. That was part of it. But the observers were mostly stunned to watch God fill the bottle of olive oil over and over to the very same level. This is what I call a creative miracle!

God Multiplies the Loaves

The night God repeatedly filled the bottle with oil is not the only time I have seen that kind of miracle. It is easy for God to multiply food. Remember when Jesus blessed the bread and fed the 5,000 men, plus women and children? (See Matt. 14:21). This happens today.

One night I was preaching at a conference for Global Harvest Ministries, founded by Peter and Doris Wagner. A friend, Tommy Tenney, had brought three loaves of bread from Bart Pierce's Rock Church in Baltimore, Maryland. Rock Church had been having an unusual visitation called the bread of His presence.

The three loaves were in the prayer room all day. A friend teased that they had been micro-waved in God's power all day. That night I preached on Jesus and Bethany, which means "the house of bread." The point of the message was found in the passage in Psalm 37:25, which reads, "I've been young and now am old; yet I have not seen the righteous forsaken, Nor his descendants begging for bread."

During the service, I had requested that the loaves of bread be placed at the front of the room. I had privately petitioned the Lord to allow the three loaves to multiply so that everyone in the sanctuary could have a piece. There were three thousand people in attendance that night. The place was packed.

At the end of my message, I split the loaves in half and gave them to some of my friends. They like to tease me that I come up with these ideas and then they have to do the work. Obviously, they know that God really does the work.

The bread did not stop multiplying until people came back for a second piece.

As Chuck Pierce, Dutch Sheets and others moved among the crowd, having each person take a piece of the bread, I occasionally asked, "Is there bread in the house?" The men would lift up the chunks of bread to show there was, indeed, still bread left. After everyone had taken a piece, there was still bread left. We then called to the front representatives of nations outside the United States, and people from 13 different countries broke off a piece of bread to take home. The bread did not stop multiplying until people came back for a second piece and then it was gone. What a symbol that God will always provide for His children.

Many people have told me how God has multiplied food when they had extra people eating in their homes. I have also seen this happen in my home while ladling soup for surprise guests.

How Does the Anointing Affect Wonders?

God is a creative God. There are many different ways that He uses people, and it is important to understand the specific ways He wants to use you. This is particularly true for wonders. As I noted earlier, I have found that the specialty that God uses me in is creative miracles, particularly through the use of word of knowledge. I see more people healed simply by announcing from the platform what God is doing than by laying hands on a thousand people. I am grateful because it also uses tremendously less spiritual energy to minister in that fashion.

This might be a good point to go into further depth about what happens when ministering under the anointing and how it affects the person it flows through, although I explained some of this earlier.

People Are Slain in the Spirit
The virtue of God is rather like electricity. This is why, at times, when someone is prayed for, the person receiving will either fall under the power or jump back as though struck. Kathryn Kuhlman explained falling under the power or "slain in the spirit" in this manner:

All I can believe is that our spiritual beings are not wired for Gods full power, and when we plug into that power, we just can't survive it. We are wired for low voltage; God is high voltage through the Holy Spirit.[4]

There are various biblical passages that describe falling under the power, such as Daniel 8:17 and John 18:6 (when the Roman soldiers and temple guards came to take Jesus away in the garden). When the soldiers and guards said they were seeking Jesus of Nazareth, He replied, "I am He." As Jesus uttered His poignant response, all of the soldiers and guards fell to the ground. Falling under the power truly is a wonder.

Earlier in this book, I recounted my first experience of being slain in the spirit, which happened at a church in Los Angeles. Later, in my early days of ministry, I found that flowing under the anointing tired me out physically. I would preach at a weekend retreat, then during the week I would take my children to school, go home and sleep for hours. I simply could not take that much power flowing through me without needing considerable rest.

Other people who flow in an anointing have told me similar things. I have also heard that one hour of preaching is like eight hours of physical labor. I believe that. However, as with physical labor, you can build up your spiritual stamina. With time, I have developed more endurance. As of this writing, I have been traveling around the world for 22 years; because of my increased stamina, I can now do more under the anointing and preach for longer periods of time.

Can the Anointing Flow Through Shoes?

The anointing will saturate physical places and even apparel. I wrote about this in the chapter *Does Dry Cleaning Hurt the Anointing?* One rather humorous example of this happened to me when I was preaching in a stadium in Mar del Plata.

We were in Argentina with Ed Silvoso and his Harvest Evangelism team, and I had preached the night before. The service was glorious, the stadium packed, and many people were being healed as the glory of God swept through the building. Hundreds of people fell under the power at one time.

The morning after this powerful visitation, I saw a friend of mind named Larry Jackson. "Cindy," Larry said, "Can I have a pair of your shoes? Even an old pair?" I looked at him in a puzzled and amused fashion. "Larry," I quipped, "we don't wear the same size and, *no*, you cannot have a pair of my shoes!"

He laughed and said, "You don't know what happened last night during the meeting, do you?" "Well, no I don't," I shot back with a laugh. He went on with a grin to relate how I had taken off my shoes when I started to pray for the crowds and had left them on the platform. A person walking across the stage tripped over my shoes and promptly fell under the power.

The platform was huge and people could easily walk underneath it. In fact, we had intercessors under the platform walking up and down praying at all times during this and similar meetings. We called them our "spiritual nuclear plant."

Larry proceeded to relate how a prayer warrior, having seen the result of the person bumping into my shoes, had gently picked them up and tiptoed downstairs with them. As he carefully touched people with the shoes, the result was the same for each one—they all fell under the power of God! When they were finished with my shoes, they quietly snuck back up to the platform and placed them in the exact position I had left them. I never knew they were missing! I suppose if handkerchiefs taken from the body of Paul could heal, then God could use old shoes, too (see Acts 19:12).

God Moves Everywhere

While there are many miracles that we have seen in meetings, I want to close with one that was rather dramatic and is emblematic of what

God can do anywhere at any time.

A Boy Comes Back to Life

One of the greatest tests of my faith came when we were doing healing meetings in Lahore, Pakistan. The meetings had been advertised widely. The rest of the team had gone before me to intercede and prepare the way. While alone in the hotel room, it seemed as if the principalities over the nation had discovered I was alone. Voices spoke in my head and shouted, "There will be no miracles tonight!"

I had heard stories of meetings in India where miracles were advertised and none manifested and people in the crowd threw stones and tried to kill the preachers. All these things piled around me as I paced the floor. Finally in anguish I cried out to the Lord, "God, I am going to do what I can do. I will go to the meeting and preach the gospel, and then you do what you can do!"

Upon arriving I was delighted to see the way in which my hosts had prepared the site for the meeting. Heavy Persian rugs were strewn across the platform, and as I came in my hosts requested that I preach with my shoes off. (This to a girl from Texas was heaven itself!) There was a tent overhead that partially covered the people. Our friends Iqbal and Kundan Massey, the founders of Campus Crusade for Christ there in Pakistan, had done a magnificent job preparing for the event.

One key that we have learned through the years in doing healing meetings is that we ask God to start the meeting with a notable miracle—someone getting up out of a wheelchair, the blind seeing, or something like that. After that happens, people run to the meetings to be healed.

All of a sudden, right in the middle of the worship, a man ran out of the crowd. He came to the platform and requested to speak. He stood up and the people looked at him in hushed silence. "I'm a Muslim," he said. "I am not a follower of Jesus Christ. I am a beggar and have had many afflictions. In fact, I dragged myself to this meeting tonight because I have heard that the Name of Jesus produced miracles. During the singing I suddenly found that I had strength in my legs and I jumped up and could walk!"

As we looked at the man, it was apparent that he had some kind of skin disorder as well because we could see scabs forming on his face as the skin disorder was being healed.

The next night he gave his life to Jesus and came up to testify again. This time his skin was as smooth as a baby's. He was totally and completely restored. After that incident many other people were healed.

The greatest wonder of the night and one that the team who came with me, as well as people in the crowd, pressed in for was a small 8-year-old boy. His father had brought him to the meeting from the hospital along with the boy's doctor because the boy had been given no hope to live. Even after I prayed for him, the child died, which was verified by his doctor. As I kept praying for others, I encouraged our team to keep praying and not give up on the child. They warred in the heavens for the life of that beautiful but emaciated child. Before long, the father brought the child to me alive! Evidently the boy had coughed, taken a breath, and had come back to life! Just like in the Bible I exhorted the father to take the child home to get something to eat. We received an email later that stated that the child was healthy and well and running around having a great time in life.

The Anointing Is In You, Too

An important point to note here is that the anointing is not just in me—it is in you also. The Bible says that those who believe will lay hands on the sick and they will recover (see Mark 16:18). If you have hands and you believe, you can pray for the sick and they *will* recover. I started out with a small measure of faith for miracles, then prayed for larger and larger groups and saw more and more answers. God works through every believer and He wants to work through you, too. He is looking for hungry, willing, obedient hearts to believe His Word.

God has done so many wonderful wonders through the years of our ministry, Generals International, but they all started from small mustard seeds of faith. Faith is always in the red. We have found that every time we get comfortable with believing for a certain amount of money, God asks us to believe for something more. Each new challenge requires more faith than the last one took. What is a big thing to believe for today is a small thing to believe for tomorrow, and God is always stretching us in our faith.

Jesus Christ is, indeed, the same yesterday, today and forever (see Heb. 13:8). He is the great I am, not the great I was. God wants to flow through you in the area of wonders. Every day should be a supernatural adventure with God. People all around you are hungry to know that God's power is real. I encourage you to have faith to step into the supernatural realm and walk in it daily.

Have fun in this! Each day look for opportunities to have adventures in the Holy Spirit. Your life will never be the same, and some of you will write books telling the amazing tales of God's wondrous power.

Your Holy Spirit Adventures

Have you ever felt the anointing of the Holy Spirit flow through you or see it flow through someone else? Write down the details, including how you felt when this happened.

Make a list of the wonders that you want to see God perform in your life. Write down a prayer asking God for these wonders and repeat it often. Then come back to this page and note when you see each wonder happen!

AFLAME FOR GOD

By Smith Wigglesworth

Christ said to his disciples just before he ascended, "Ye shall receive power, after the Holy Ghost is come upon you: and ye shall be witnesses unto me" (Acts 1:8). On the day of Pentecost, he sent the power as promised. And the remainder of the Acts of the Apostles tells of the witnessing of these Spirit-filled disciples, the Lord working with them and confirming the word with signs following.

The Lord Jesus is just the same today. The anointing is just the same. The Pentecostal experience is just the same. And we are to look for like results as set forth in Luke's record of what happened in the days of the early church.

John the Baptist said concerning Jesus, "He shall baptize you with the Holy Ghost, and *with* fire" (Matthew 3:11b). God's ministers are to be a flame of fire—a perpetual flame, a constant fire, a continual burning, shining lights. God has nothing less than for us to be flames. We must have a living faith in God, a belief that his great might and power may flame through us until our whole lives are energized by his power.

When the Holy Ghost comes he comes to enable us to show forth Jesus Christ in all his glory, to make him known as the one who heals today as in the days of old. The baptism in the Spirit enables us to preach as they did at the beginning, through the power of the Holy Ghost sent down from heaven and with the manifestation of the gifts of the Spirit. Oh, if we would only let the Lord work in us, melting us until a new mandate arises, moved with his compassion!

God was wonderfully with me as I traveled by ship from Egypt to Italy. Every hour I was conscious of his blessed presence. When a man on board suddenly collapsed, his wife was terribly alarmed, along with everybody else. Some said that he was about to expire. But I saw it was just a glorious opportunity for the power of God to be manifested.

Oh, what it means to be a flame of fire, to be indwelt by the living Christ! We are behind time if we have to pray for power when an occasion like that comes, or if we have to wait until we feel a sense of his presence. The Lord's promise was, "You shall receive power after the Holy Ghost is come upon you." And if we will believe, the power of God will be always manifested when there is a definite need. When you exercise your faith, you will find you have a greater power than that in the world. Oh, to be awakened out of unbelief into a place of daring for God on the authority of his blessed Book!

So right there on board that ship, in the name of Jesus, I rebuked the devil. To the astonishment of the man's wife and the man himself, he was able to stand. He said, "What is this? It is going all over me. I have never felt anything like this before." From the top of his head to the soles of his feet the power of God shook him. God has given us authority over all the power of the devil. Oh, that we may live in the place where we realize this always!

More Than Conquerors

Christ, who is the express image of God, has come to our human weaknesses, to change them and us into divine likeness, to make us partakers of the divine nature, so that by the power of his might we may not only overcome but also rejoice in the fact that we are more than conquerors.

God wants you to know by experience what it means to be more than a conqueror. The baptism in the Holy Spirit has come for nothing less than to empower you, to give you the very power that Christ himself had, so that you, a yielded vessel, may continue the same type of ministry that Jesus had when he walked this earth in the days of his flesh. He purposes that you should come behind in no gift. There are gifts of healing and the working of miracles, but they must be apprehended. There is the gift of faith by the same Spirit which you are to receive.

The need in the world today is that we should be burning and shining lights to reflect the glory of Christ. We cannot do this with a cold, indifferent experience, and we never shall. His servants are to be flames of fire. Christ came that we might have life, and life more abundantly. And we are to give that life to others, to be ministers of the life and power and healing virtue of Jesus Christ wherever we go.

Some years ago I was in Ceylon (Sri Lanka). In one place my fellow workers complained, "Four days is not much to give us." "No," I said "but it is a good share." They said to me, "We are not touching the people here at all." I asked, "Can you have a meeting early in the morning, at eight o'clock?" They said they would. So I instructed them, "Tell all the mothers who want their babies to be healed to come, and all the people over seventy to come, and after that we hope to give an address to the people to make them ready for the baptism in the Spirit." It would have done you good to see the four hundred mothers coming at eight o'clock with their babies, and then to see the 150 old people with their white hair coming to be healed.

We need to have something more than smoke to touch the people; we need to be a burning fire for God. His ministers must be flames of fire. In those days in Ceylon thousands came out to hear the Word of God. I believe there were about three thousand people crying for mercy at once. It was a great sight. From that first morning the meetings grew to such an extent that I would estimate every time some five to six thousand gathered, while I had to preach in a temperature of 110 degrees. Then I had to pray for these people who were sick. But I can tell you, a flame of fire can do anything. Things change in the fire.

This was Pentecost in our midst. But here's what moved me more than anything else: there were hundreds who tried to touch me, they were so impressed with the power of God that was present. And many testified that with that touch they were healed. It was not that there was any virtue in me. The people's faith was exercised as it was in Jerusalem when they believed Peter's shadow would heal them.

You can receive something in three minutes that you can carry with you into glory. What do you want? Is anything too hard for God? God can meet you now. God sees inwardly; he knows all about you. Nothing is hidden from him. And he can satisfy the soul and give you a spring of eternal blessing that will carry you right through.[1]

ENDNOTES

Introduction

1. In recent years, especially among participants in The Call movement, something called the Nazirite vow has emerged. Following the example of Job, who made a covenant with his eyes to not look lustfully at a woman (see Job: 31:1), and Paul, who cut his hair (see Acts 18:18), young men and women take a vow of "separation to the Lord" (Acts 6:2). For more information see Pete Greig, *The Vision and the Vow: Re-Discovering Life and Grace* (Lake Mary, FL: Relevant Books, 2004), pp. 120-121.

Chapter One

1. "Paranormal" means "something that is not scientifically explainable" (*Merriam-Webster's Ninth New Collegiate Dictionary*, s.v. "paranormal").
2. C. Peter Wagner, *Acts of the Holy Spirit* (Ventura, CA: Regal Books, 2000), p. 104.
3. Jack Hayford, *The Beauty of Spiritual Language* (Nashville, TN: Thomas Nelson Publishers, 1992), p. 92.
4. Ibid., pp. 95-96.
5. Claudio Freidzon, *Holy Spirit, I Hunger for You* (Lake Mary, FL: Creation House, 1997), p. 63.
6 Cindy Jacobs, *Deliver Us from Evil* (Ventura, CA: Regal Books, 2001), pp. 211-216.
7 Wagner, *Acts of the Holy Spirit*, p. 104.

Chapter Two

1. C. Peter Wagner, *How to Have a Healing Ministry in Any Church* (Ventura, CA: Regal Books, 1988), p. 170.
2. Jack Deere, *Surprised by the Power of the Spirit* (Grand Rapids, MI: Zondervan Publishing House, 1993), p. 124.

Chapter Three

1. C. Peter Wagner, *Your Spiritual Gifts* (Ventura, CA: Regal Books, 1994), p. 96.
2. Roxanne Brant, *How to Test: Prophecy and Preaching, Guidance* (O'Brien, FL: Roxanne Brant Ministries, 1981), p. 81.
3. I further explain this biblical concept in two of my books, *The Voice of God* (Ventura, CA: Regal Books, 1995) and *Deliver Us from Evil* (Ventura, CA: Regal Books, 2001).
4. For a good reference book to help in this area, please see John and Mark Sandford, *A Comprehensive Guide to Deliverance and Inner Healing* (Grand Rapids, MI: Chosen Books, 1992).
5. For those of you who are unfamiliar with how to break curses, I recommend my book *Deliver Us from Evil*.

Chapter Four

1. Evelyn Hamon, phone conversation with Cindy Jacobs, December 2003.
2. In you suffer from diabetes or another ailment that requires prescription medication, please do not stop taking your medicine after being prayed for unless you have either a doctor's permission to stop or solid evidence that you are completely healed. Evelyn Hamon is still checking her blood sugar levels to make sure that she is fine without medicine and she watches her diet.
3. For more information on the relationship of unforgiveness and trauma to issues of healing, read Charles Kraft, *Deep Wounds, Deep Healing* (Ann Arbor, MI: Servant Publications, 1993) and Ché Ahn, *How to Pray for Healing* (Ventura, CA: Regal Books, 2003).
4. *Strong's Exhaustive Concordance*, no. 1982.
5. Ché Ahn, *How to Pray for Healing* (Ventura, CA: Regal Books, 2003), n.p.
6. C. Peter Wagner, *Your Spiritual Gifts* (Ventura, CA: Regal Books, 1994), p. 210.
7. Francis MacNutt, *Healing* (Notre Dame, IN: Ave Maria Press, 1999), p. 249.

Chapter Five

1. Roberts Liardon, *God's Generals* (Tulsa, OK: Albury Publishing, 1996), p. 183.
2. Ibid., p. 183.
3. "More Spokane Facts," *Spokane Area Economic Development Council.* http://www.spokaneedc.org/about/spokane_facts.php (accessed February 1, 2005).
4. Maria Woodworth-Etter, *Signs and Wonders* (Tulsa, OK: Harrison House, n.d.), p. 29.
5. Ibid., p. 32.
6. Ibid., p. 40.
7. Ibid., p. 63.
8. Smith Wigglesworth, *Ever Increasing Faith* (Springfield, MO: Radiant Books, 1974), p. 5.
9. Roberts Liardon, *God's Generals*, p. 20.
10. Ibid., p. 211.
11. Ibid., p. 215.
12. Wigglesworth, *Ever Increasing Faith*, p. 83.
13. Daniel Mark Epstein, *Sister Aimee: The Life of Aimee Semple McPherson* (Orlando, FL: Harcourt Brace and Company, 1993), p. 10.
14. Aimee Semple McPherson, *The Story of My life* (Waco, TX: Word, Inc., 1973), p. 75.

Chapter Six

1. Smith Wigglesworth, *Ever Increasing Faith* (Springfield, MO: Radiant Books, 1971), pp. 104-105.
2. Donald Posterski, *Reinventing Evangelism* (Downers Grove, IL: InterVarsity Press, 1989), p. 28.
3. Ed Silvoso has said this many times in many venues.

4. Pete Greig and Dave Roberts, *Red Moon Rising* (Lake Mary, FL: Relevant Books, 2003), pp. 2-3.
5. Ibid., pp. 196, 198-199.

Chapter Seven
1. Billy Graham, *Angels* (Dallas, TX: Word Publishing, 1994), p. 185.
2. Ibid., pp. 4-5.
3. Clement of Alexandria, quoted at "The Coptic Church and Dogmas," *Coptic Orthodox Church Network*. http://www.copticchurch.net/topics/thecopticchurch/church3-2.html (accessed Feb 4, 2005).
4. Pseudo-Dionysius, source unknown.
5. C. Peter Wagner, *Acts of the Holy Spirit* (Ventura, CA: Regal Books, 2000), p. 275.
6. Graham, *Angels*, p. 181.

Chapter Eight
1. Roberts Liardon, *God's Generals* (Tulsa, OK: Albury Publishing, 1996), p. 506.
2. Dick Eastman, *Dick Eastman on Prayer* (Toronto, ON: Global Christian Publishers, 1989), pp. 156-157.
3. Dick Eastman, *The Purple Pig and Other Miracles* (Monroeville, PA: Whitaker House, 1974), p. 125.
4. Liardon, *God's Generals*, p. 296.

Appendix
1. Smith Wigglesworth, "Aflame for God." *Pentecostal Evangel* (October 17, 1942), p. 5. Used by permission.

RECOMMENDED READING

Ahn, Ché. *How to Pray for Healing.* Ventura, CA: Regal Books, 2004.

———. *Into the Fire*: Ventura, CA: Renew Books, 1998.

Bosworth, F. F. *Christ the Healer.* Grand Rapids, MI: Fleming H. Revell Company, 2000.

Buckingham, Jamie. *Kathryn Kuhlman: Daughter of Destiny.* North Brunswick, NJ: Bridge-Logos Publishers, 1999.

Deere, Jack. *Surprised by the Voice of God.* Grand Rapids, MI: Zondervan Publishing House, 1996.

Finney, Charles. *Holy Spirit Revivals: How You Can Experience the Joy of Living in God's Power.* New Kensington, PA: Whitaker House, 1999.

Freidzon, Claudio. *Holy Spirit, I Hunger for You.* Lake Mary, FL: Creation House Books, 1997.

Goll, Jim W. *The Beginner's Guide to Hearing God.* Ventura, CA: Regal Books, 2004.

Graham, Billy. *Angels.* Dallas, TX: Word Publishing, 1994.

Hamon, Bill. *Apostles, Prophets and the Coming Moves of God.* Shippensburg, PA: DestinyImage Books, 1997.

Hamon, Jane. *Dreams and Visions.* Santa Rosa Beach, FL: Christian International Family Church, 1997.

Hayford, Jack W. *Living the Spirit-Formed Life.* Ventura, CA: Regal Books, 2001.

——. *The Beauty of Spiritual Language*. Nashville, TN: Nelson Books, 1996.

Hinn, Benny. *Good Morning Holy Spirit*. Nashville, TN: Thomas Nelson Publishers, 1990.

Jacobs, Cindy. *The Voice of God*. Ventura, CA: Regal Books, 1995.

Lee, Joyce, and Warner, Wayne E., eds. *The Essential Smith Wigglesworth*. Ventura, CA: Regal Books, 1999.

Liardon, Roberts, ed. *God's Generals*. Tulsa, OK: Albury Publishing, 1996.

——. *John G. Lake*. Tulsa, OK: Albury Publishing, 1999.

——. *Smith Wigglesworth*. Tulsa, OK: Albury Publishing, 1996.

MacNutt, Francis, *Healing*. Notre Dame, IN: Ave Maria Press, 1999.

McPherson, Aimee Semple, *The Story of My Life*. Waco, TX: Word Books, 1973.

——. *This Is That*. Los Angeles: Echo Park Evangelistic Association, n.d.

Pierce, Chuck D., and Sytsema, Rebecca W. *Possessing Your Inheritance*. Ventura, CA: Regal Books, 1999.

Prince, Derek. *How to Judge Prophecy*. Fort Lauderdale, FL: Derek Prince Publications, 1971.

Roberts, Oral. *Expect a Miracle*. Nashville, TN: Thomas Nelson Publishers, 1995.

Sheets, Dutch. *The River of God*. Ventura, CA: Regal Books, 1998.

Sherrer, Quin, and Garlock, Ruthanne. *The Beginner's Guide to Receiving the Holy Spirit*. Ventura, CA: Regal Books, 2002.

Silvoso, Ed. *That None Should Perish*. Ventura, CA: Regal Books, 1994.

Synan, Vinson. *Voices of Pentecost*. Ann Arbor, MI: Vine Books, 2003.

Wagner, C. Peter. *Acts of the Holy Spirit*. Ventura, CA: Regal Books, 2000.

——. *Your Spiritual Gifts*. Ventura, CA: Regal Books, 1994.

Wentroble, Barbara. *Prophetic Intercession*. Ventura, CA: Regal Books, 1999.

Wigglesworth, Smith. *The Anointing of His Spirit.* Ventura, CA: Regal Books, 1994.

Woodworth-Etter, Maria. *Signs and Wonders.* Tulsa, OK: Harrison House Books, 1916.

INDEX

Methodist, 97, 101
Miami, Florida, 162
Michigan, 90
monster, 56
Moscow, 142
Moses, 11, 87
moves of God, 86
Musch, Leslyn, 130
Muslim, 171
N
Nelson's Bible Dictionary, 145
New Lisbon, Ohio, 94
O
obedience, 43, 46, 73, 161, 172
occult, 64, 77
oil, 74-75, 164-165
Ontario, Canada, 103
overshadowing, 78
P
paralyzed, 47
paranormal, 14
patriarchs, 11, 88
peace, 17-18, 66, 159
Pentecostal, 11, 25, 94, 100
Phoebe, 164
Pickford, Mary, 106
Pierce, Bart, 165
Pierce, Cal, 90-91
Pierce, Chuck, 157, 166
Pierce, Michelle, 90-91
Pierson, Paul, 44
Pierson, Sara, 44
Pierson, Steve, 44
plague, 89
poisoned water, 163-164
Portuguese settlement, 104
Possessing the Gates of the Enemy, 67
Posterski, Donald, 120
praise, 80-81
prayer, 28, 64, 66
    24-hour, 91-92, 106, 123, 125
    cloths, 71-72
    renouncing, 64
    soaking, 82-83
    warrior, 125
preternatural influence, 78
prophecy
    evangelism, 111-115, 118-119, 123, 125-126
    movement, 73

prophets, 163
Pseudo-Dionysius, 136
Purple Pig and Other Miracles: Cripples Walk, Floods Are Stopped, the Sick Are Healed, 160
Q
questions for God, 16-17
Quinn, Anthony, 106
R
race, 87-88
radio, 105
Raphael, 143
Rasputin Grigory, 142
realm
    earthly, 15, 87
    heavenly, 87
    spiritual, 36, 52, 57-58, 60, 66
    supernatural, 60
Red Moon Rising, 123-124
Red Sea, 156-158
Reformation anointing, 93
reformers, societal, 93
rejection, 62-63
relationships, 93
    sabotage, 63
Resistencia, 77
Revelation, 34, 76
revival, 86, 95, 97-98, 112, 140
    in the nations, 95
rheumatism, 90
Rio de Janeiro, 140
rivers of living water, 39
Roberts, Oral, 106, 152
Romans, 123, 168
root, 75, 91
Russia, 142
S
Saints movement, 101-102
Salford, Ontario, Canada, 103
Salvation Army, 90, 99
Samaria, 16-17
Sandford, John, 159
Sandford, Paula, 159
Santa Rosa Beach, Florida, 73
Sarah, 87
Satan, 35
    Satanic, 55, 60
    Satan's kingdom, 66
schools, 102
Scripture, 88

GENERALS INTERNATIONAL

Achieving Societal Transformation Through Intercession and the Prophetic

Other Books and Series by Cindy Jacobs

Possessing the Gates of the Enemy (Baker Books)
The Voice of God (Gospel Light)
Women of Destiny (Gospel Light)
Spirit Led Woman Devotional Bible

Deliver Us From Evil (Audio series)
Women of Destiny (Audio and Video series)
Societal Reformation and Transformation (Audio and Video series, 7 sessions)
Prophets, Prophecy and the Prophetic (Audio series, 12 sessions)
Wealth (Audio, single)

For these products, visit our online store at
www.generals.org

FOR MORE INFORMATION ABOUT THE
MINISTRY OF CINDY JACOBS,
call: (972) 576-8887 fax: (972) 576-8899
e-mail: generals@generals.org
Or mail to: P.O. Box 340
Red Oak, TX 75154

MORE OF THE BEST
FROM CINDY JACOBS

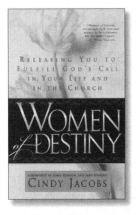

Women of Destiny
Releasing You to Fulfill God's Call
in Your Life and in the Church
ISBN 08307.18648
VHS • Approx. 105 min.
UPC 607135.003861

Deliver Us from Evil
Putting a Stop to the Occult Influences Invading
Your Home and Community
ISBN 08307.28007

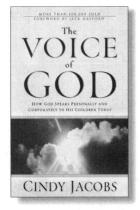

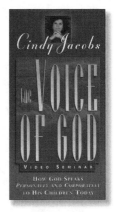

The Voice of God
How God Speaks Personally and
Corporately to His Children Today
Cindy Jacobs
ISBN 08307.36387

The Voice of God
How God Speaks Personally and
Corporately to His Children Today
VHS • Approx. 240 min.
UPC 607135.001195